Information and Communication Technology and Small and Medium Sized Enterprises

Information and Communication Technology and Small and Medium Sized Enterprises: From Theory to Practice

Edited by

Diane Poulin and Sébastien Tran

CAMBRIDGE
SCHOLARS
PUBLISHING

Information and Communication Technology and Small and Medium Sized Enterprises:
From Theory to Practice, Edited by Diane Poulin and Sébastien Tran

This book first published 2010

Cambridge Scholars Publishing

12 Back Chapman Street, Newcastle upon Tyne, NE6 2XX, UK

British Library Cataloguing in Publication Data
A catalogue record for this book is available from the British Library

ISBN (10): 1-4438-1326-5, ISBN (13): 978-1-4438-1326-6

TABLE OF CONTENTS

ACKNOWLEDGEMENTS

Without the dedicated work of the following chapter authors, this book would not exist: François Bergeron, Sébastien Caisse, Luca Canetta, Naoufel Cheikhrouhou, Yan Cimon, Sophie D'Amours, Jean-Marc Frayret, Rémy Glardon, Pierre Hadaya, Hedi Kaffel, Rafa Kouki, Benoit Montreuil, Robert Pellerin, Jean-François Rougès, and Constance Van Horne. Warm thanks are due to the experts participating in the Delphi study, the managers and the companies participating in the case studies and all the survey respondents.

For their invaluable financial support to the research, we gratefully acknowledge the Canada Economic Development for Quebec Regions and the Natural Sciences and Engineering Research Council of Canada (Government of Canada), the Ministère du Développement économique, de l'innovation et de l'Exportation (MDEIE), Emploi Québec and the Fonds de recherche sur la société et la culture (Government of Quebec), the Swiss Innovation and Promotion Agency (CTI), and the Research start-up Fund at Université Laval.

We would also like to thank the Interuniversity Research Centre on Enterprise Networks, Logistics and Transportation (CIRRELT), the FOR@C Research Consortium, the Canada Research Chair in Enterprise Engineering, the Laboratory for Production Management and Processes at EPFL (Ecole Polytechnique Fédérale de Lausanne), and the Centre de recherche industrielle Québec (CRIQ) for their daily support.

Many others have contributed their knowledge and skills to various aspects of the production process: Eric Landry, Fatima Zahra Barrane, Yvonne Badulescu, Marianne Cachin. We are grateful to Mary Parlange for proofreading the book, and Eric Landry for preparing the index.

INTRODUCTION

As defined by the Organization for Economic Cooperation and Development (OECD), SMEs are companies employing less than 250 persons. Generally representing between 95% and 98% of companies worldwide (Marchesnay 2003) and a relatively significant portion of most macro-economic indicators regardless of activity sector (industry or services), they play a major role in the economies of most countries. Given the diversity of their activities and their positions in the various sectors and value chains, they form a very heterogeneous group, but they are nonetheless a driving force in terms of innovation and entrepreneurial dynamics. Despite the advantages offered by their size and their often more flexible and reactive structure, however, they can experience problems with economic competitiveness both internationally and with large companies in their activity sector.

The mid-1990s marked a clear discontinuity in competitive dynamics and the start of a period of innovation in Information and Communications Technologies (ICT). The Internet and enterprise software applications, such as Enterprise Resource Planning (ERP) and Customer Relationship Management (CRM), became practical tools for business. The Internet represented a major disruptive innovation for a broad set of industries, and generally ICT are widespread in most countries around the world

In the 1990s research began to report a positive relationship between ICT investment and productivity, provided there were investments in both information technology and organization. For example, corporate investments in ICT surged during this time from about $3.500 spent per worker in 1994 to about $8.000 in 2005, according to the U.S Bureau of Economic Analysis (BEA). Another study of Canadian manufacturing companies (plants) with ten or more employees (excluding food processing plants) drawn from Statistics Canada's Business Register shows that those with high productivity growth are more likely to be using more advanced ICT (Baldwin 2002). In an ever-changing and dynamic world, the adoption of ICT across the globe has permanently altered the rules of the game and the expectations of the new digital and inter-connected economies. Productivity is one of the indicators demonstrating that ICT is a key factor by which firms can enhance their competitiveness.

SMEs are increasingly aware of the positive impact that ICT can have as these technologies spread through their organizations. Among the different tools for SME development and competitiveness, ICT have become widespread in every activity sector over the last several decades. Behind this very general acronym hides a multitude of technologies — for example, computers, Internet, groupware, Electronic Data Interchange (EDI) and Enterprise Resource Planning (ERP)—that are supposed to improve the performance of organizations.

One explanation for the pervasiveness of ICT is that these technologies theoretically permit gains in productivity, particularly in terms of transactions and coordination. The strategies implemented by companies to encourage ICT and electronic commerce are theoretically supposed to improve company performance through cost reductions and differentiation strategies. However, ICT provide only a partial explanation for performance improvement in most studies. As Solow's Paradox[1] indicates, measuring this performance gain has proven quite difficult and subject to debate.

Historically, large companies were the first to set up ICT (Antonelli 1986), both for organizational reasons (e.g., to maintain links with subsidiaries, to coordinate distant sites) and economic reasons (e.g., to better integrate processes, to automate data exchanges with key suppliers). In order to accomplish these goals, these pioneering companies had to restructure their operational processes, modify their organizational structures and redefine their core activities and their positions in the value chains. Thus, digitalizing a company's internal and external processes necessitates changes in organization and management. These changes often generate costs and risks that are proportionately greater for SMEs, which may also lack expertise and knowledge, leading to longer ICT implementation and appropriation phases.

The structural transformations in the various sectors have led to a greater organizational interdependence between firms, especially between

---

[1] In 1987, Robert Solow, Nobel laureate in economics, stated in "We Had Better Watch Out," in the *New York Review of Books* (July 12, 1987):"You can see the computer age everywhere these days, except in the productivity statistics". This economist thus affirmed that the business world's massive investments in ICT didn't lead to significant gains in productivity.

large companies and SMEs, which are often sub-contractors providing goods and/or services. This is particularly true of transformations that, applying the concepts of vertical disintegration or networks, have pushed companies to re-center on their core activities and to modularize their production systems. The external pressure of large companies and clients has led numerous SMEs to set up ICT, especially in industrial sectors, as will be seen in the various chapters of this book.

Internet technologies are assumed to play a major role in the simultaneous processes of company disintegration and reinforcement of the interorganizational relationships between companies. According to OECD surveys, SMEs are increasing their use of ICT. A Eurostat survey of electronic commerce indicated that, by the end of 2000/beginning of 2001, nine out of ten SMEs were equipped with computers. Thus, it appears that the Internet has become a widely used tool in small companies. Although the use of the Internet in large companies is more commonplace, the Internet use gap between large and small companies is quickly disappearing. In most OECD countries, with a few exceptions, the Internet penetration rate in medium-sized companies (50-249 employees) has reached, or exceeded, the levels observed in larger companies (250+ employees), with rates over 80%.

The arrival of ICT may play a role in restoring competitiveness, since these technologies are also a factor in relaxing the constraints specific to SMEs. ICT makes a number of services possible in a large range of processes and transactions within and between companies. Internally, ICT applications can improve knowledge and information management practices; they can also allow more rapid and more reliable transactions between businesses (B2B) and between businesses and consumers (B2C). They are equally quite effective in improving external business communications and service quality for both new and existing clients. They also appear to be a source of competitive advantage for SMEs under certain conditions.

Few studies in the literature have focused on the ways that SMEs can use ICT to improve and defend their competitive positions. This book provides a synthesis of the advantages of ICT for SMEs. Seven chapters illustrate the technologies used in such companies, often with concrete examples. Each of these chapters provides a theoretical and/or practical view of the way that SMEs can use ICT.

The first chapter, written by Sébastien Caisse, Sophie D'Amours, Benoit Montreuil and Diane Poulin, proposes a conceptual framework with a definition of ICT and a typology for various ICT found in the literature. Readers are invited to question what they know and assume about these ICT and SMEs. The framework proposed in this chapter plays a key role in questioning, categorizing and uncovering the broader undercurrents at work. The authors apply their framework to the Manufacturing Business Technology's 2007 Global 100, a compilation limited to a hundred entries, designed to encourage global players providing applications for the manufacturing and supply chain markets. They also propose a new way to categorize information technologies in the context of small and medium size manufacturing firms, with the aim of identifying emerging trends. Information and communication design may turn out to be the most crucial aspect of manufacturing.

In chapter two, Sophie D'Amours, Benoit Montreuil, Diane Poulin and Jean-François Rougès present a review of the literature about the links between SME performance and ICT use, as well as the variables that influence these links. Research has highlighted several advantages of ICT use in SMEs, but many questions remain, particularly regarding the systemic vision of performance improvements linked to other factors. Based on their literature review, the authors propose a 6-variable analysis framework that examines the links between ICT use and SME performance.

In chapter three, François Bergeron, Yan Cimon, Diane Poulin and Jean-François Rougès present their synthesis of the literature about the *strategic alignment* concept, which is an issue for companies seeking to improve their performance. Although many researchers have examined this concept, theoretical and methodological problems remain. After defining the concept of strategic alignment and presenting different methodological approaches for measuring this alignment, the authors demonstrate, through studies related to the strategic alignment of ICT and performance, that the results have been contradictory, revealing certain paradoxes.

In the fourth chapter, Luca Canetta, Naoufel Cheikhrouhou and Rémy Glardon identify the attributes influencing customer willingness to adopt e-purchasing practices and formalize the relationships between the attributes identified. They aim to provide a description of e-purchasing adoption characteristics by applying Diffusion of Innovation (DOI) models. Identifying customer e-purchasing behavior is essential for companies thinking about introducing new e-sales channels, because this allows them to estimate the e-sales figures that can potentially be reached by targeting these customers.

With its origins in Web-based tools and other interorganizational information systems (IOISs) such as B2B e-commerce tools, e-collaboration now describes relationships that go beyond simple buy-and-sell transactions (Johnson and Whang 2002). Today, Web-based IOISs play a crucial role in the evolution of supply chain relationships, as because they can support a number of collaborative processes ranging from direct procurement, replenishment, delivery and design to more strategic processes such as capacity planning (Cassivi 2006). The importance of SMEs in the value chain in manufacturing sectors is such that it seems important to identify the factors that incite SMEs to collaborate electronically. In chapter 5, Pierre Hadaya and Robert Pellerin examine one of the key dimensions of supply chain collaboration: information sharing. By taking advantage of the technical capabilities of the Internet, manufacturing SMEs that are members of virtual enterprises may be able to skip the lengthy, incremental process generally required to participate in global markets. In this chapter, the authors weigh the influence of various determinants on manufacturing firms' intent to use Web-based interorganizational information systems to share inventory information with their key customers.

In the sixth chapter, Jean-Marc Frayret, Hedi Kaffel, Diane Poulin and Constance Van Horne present a concrete illustration of ICT use as a support tool for Research and Development (R&D) in SMEs. The challenges of the new global economy are numerous, and many SMEs simply do not have the necessary internal R&D capabilities to develop adequate responses to these challenges. To overcome these weaknesses, SMEs can look to universities or centers of expertise to help find solutions to these new challenges with innovative products, processes and business systems. After reviewing the literature about knowledge and technology transfers from academic-industrial research groups to industry, the authors present an exploratory case study of an example of such a research group working with the Quebec furniture industry. This case will investigate how an electronic forum was used and viewed by both researchers and members of SMEs.

In the last chapter, Rafa Kouki, Robert Pellerin and Diane Poulin focus on the antecedents of ERP assimilation. Enterprise resource planning (ERP) systems have been promoted as a critical technology in an increasingly complex and knowledge-intensive economy. Given the potential benefits that an ERP system can generate for a company and the large financial commitment that it requires, it is important to understand and investigate the determinants that facilitate the ERP assimilation process in SMEs. This chapter is based on the experience of two manufacturing companies, one large company and one SME, that have adopted an ERP system. The authors explain the different factors that facilitate or hamper ERP assimilation.

CHAPTER ONE

CONCEPTUAL POSITIONING FRAMEWORK FOR INFORMATION AND COMMUNICATION TECHNOLOGIES AIMED AT SMALL AND MEDIUM SIZED MANUFACTURERS

SÉBASTIEN CAISSE, DIANE POULIN, BENOIT MONTREUIL AND SOPHIE D'AMOURS

Introduction

In Norse mythology, Thor the god of thunder slays Jormungandr, the world-serpent that encircles the Earth, by wielding his mighty hammer called Mjolnir. Think of it as a metaphor for what happened during the 20th century, when Man's mastery of electromagnetism blossomed into the Internet, information technology and the global village. The barriers which were inherent to distance were struck down.

Information technology, Man's Mjolnir, is nothing new. Books, after all, are a human technology, and deal mostly in information. But the information technology alluded to in this chapter is quite different. Its definition is elusive, though most people associate it with circuits and code, with hardware and software, rather than with paper and leather. It is different because it is implicitly bounded by a notion of novelty, which is itself bounded by cultural relativism.

In the context of small and medium manufacturing enterprises, things get a bit more complicated. Take the example of that small local manufacturer that does not manufacture at all, and instead designs its products over the Web and subcontracts the work offshore, Mjolnir firmly planted in Jormungandr's skull. Can that organization be considered a manufacturer even though it doesn't carry out any manufacturing internally?

Information technologies (IT), small and medium enterprises, manufacturers, these are concepts that are heard so often that we take their meaning for granted. And we do the same thing with expressions such as Enterprise Resource Planning, Supply Chain Management and Computer Aided Design. We even reduce them to acronyms to feel like we know and master them better: ERP, SCM, CAD—simple concepts, really. But they are not simple. They evolve. They mean different things to different industry stakeholders. Some acronyms will survive a few years in the market, others perhaps a bit longer. Information technologies transform one another ceaselessly, and buzzwords live and die short lives.

In the following sections, readers are invited to question what they know and assume about these concepts. The use of myth as metaphor was a prelude. A new way to categorize information technologies in the context of small and medium manufacturing firms is proposed. This new framework is interesting, but is not an end in itself. Yes, the proposed framework makes sense of information technologies in a different way. But more value lies in the journey towards this new framework and in the often uncomfortable process of questioning existing forms and categories.

1. A conceptual positioning framework

What are information and communication technologies (ICT)? The question is not as innocent as it looks. What constitutes an ICT is the object of much confusion in the scientific business management literature (Rougès et al. 2007). The Organization for Economic Cooperation and Development (OECD) provides an indirect answer in its Information Technology Outlook 2008, page 30, by looking at ICT activities rather than ICTs themselves[1]:

> "ICT activities are those that "process, deliver, and display information electronically". Hence, the ICT industries are those that produce the equipment, software and services that enable those activities. Each of the top 250 firms is classified by ICT industry sector: i) communication equipment and systems; ii) electronics; iii) specialist semiconductors; iv) IT equipment and systems; v) IT services; vi) software; vii) Internet; and viii) telecommunication services. Broadcast and cable media and content

[1] See Information Technology Outlook, 2008, Organization for Economic Cooperation and Development. Last visited March 9th, 2009: http://www.oecd.org/document/20/0,3343,en_2649_33757_41892820_1_1_1_1,00.html

are excluded."

It should be noted that this OECD survey was conducted in 2006. The ICT activities that were used to identify ICT industries were based on a 1998 definition from OECD's Working Party on Indicators for the Information Society (WPIIS), later complemented by an ICT goods definition in 2003 and an ICT services definition in 2006[2]. This definition was revised in 2007 by the WPIIS for the International Standard Industrial Classification (ISIC) Revision 4[3]:

> "The following general principle (definition) is used to identify ICT economic activities (industries): The production (goods and services) of a candidate industry must primarily be intended to fulfill or enable the function of information processing and communication by electronic means, including transmission and display."

Following this OECD WPIIS document, the ICT sector comprises ICT manufacturing industries, ICT repair industries, ICT trade industries and ICT services industries, but excludes the content and media sector, although both ICT and the content and media sectors belong to the broader concept of "information economy". This definition is evolving and remains problematic for some activities. For example, the case can be made that the publishing of productivity software belongs to the ICT services sector while the publishing of multimedia software is part of the content and media sector. However, both are part of the ICT services industries, notably because ISIC recognizes only one software publishing industry that produces both types of software.

In a less structured and coherent manner, ICT producers have also devised their own ICT classification schemes. They group and advertize the ICTs they sell under labels such as *Enterprise Resource Planning* (ERP) or *Supply Chain Management* (SCM), which reflect the intended fulfillment or enabling function of the ICTs they offer. Such labels and groupings can vary from one source to the next. Moreover, some ICT producers purposefully craft new labels and acronyms for their ICTs in a bid for market differentiation. Finally, some classification schemes

---

[2] See Information Economy -- Sector Definitions Based on the International Standard Industry Classification (ISIC 4), DSTI/ICCP/IIS(2006)2/FINAL, Organisation for Economic Co-operation and Development. Last visited March 9th, 2009: http://www.oecd.org/dataoecd/49/17/38217340.pdf

[3] Idem, Annex 1.

originate from other ICT sector stakeholders. Some are industry specific, such as furniture manufacturing ICTs (Azouzi et al. 2007). Others are more inclusive, such as the five ICT families proposed by Reed Business Information's Manufacturing Business Technology magazine's Global 100 ICTs for small and medium manufacturers:

1. Product innovation (ICT meant to sustain innovation, such as computer assisted design, engineering or manufacturing software);
2. Computing infrastructure (ICT meant to enable other ICT families such as servers, computers, security software, and so forth);
3. Plant operations (ICT meant to digitize plants and equipment, such as robots and control software);
4. Enterprise/supply chain (ICT meant to enact the virtual value chain, such as radio frequency identification tags and software (RFID));
5. Business performance (ICT meant to yield business intelligence and value added knowledge).

A new way to conceptually position Enterprise Information and Communication Technologies (ICT^Es) is offered here. This classification scheme is presented as a complement to other approaches to ICT classification, and is based on making explicit certain assumptions commonly found in business management discourse. On the one hand, an enterprise is composed of ICT-using individuals. On the other hand, it is embedded in an environment providing an enabling infrastructure. As a result, it is assumed that ICT^Es exclude those ICTs which deal first and foremost with such individuals or are provided through the business's environment. If it were not so, the ICT^E landscape would in fact be the global ICT landscape in its ever-changing entirety.

A first conceptual boundary can thus be found between ICTs intended for individuals and ICT^Es. This boundary is useful to determine which ICT is meaningful to the discourse at hand. For example, knowing how to use a telephone refers to an ICT which is common to firms of every size and trade, and which permeates the whole of modern society. This ICT is conceptually outside the boundaries of ICT^Es.

A second boundary refers to the environment, involving the notion of scale. Many ICTs essential or useful to enterprises are found upstream from those intended specifically for enterprises. These include computer operating systems, satellite networks, credit card systems, and the Internet – ICTs of general interest which enable ICTs of more specific intent. To describe them all in the context of enterprises would be an exercise in futility. But at what point does the exercise cease to be futile and start to add meaning to the contextualized discourse? That is where the second boundary can be found, between ICTs presumed to be present in the business environment and useful to commerce in general, versus ICTs intended specifically for enterprises so that they may better interact with such an environment.

These two boundaries find their echo in the scientific business literature. In a contribution to knowledge-based theories of the firm, Sveiby (2001) proposed a tripartite view of a firm's knowledge transfers and conversions. Figure 1-1 adapts this view to represent an enterprise as an internal structure which encompasses conceptual spaces of knowledge transfer and conversion within itself, among competent individuals, with an external structure, and with both of these at once.

The enterprise's internal structure interacts with an external structure such as a market, an industry or an environment. It also interacts through, and among, competent individuals such as employees, investors and end users. Knowledge is transferred and transformed between and through these three poles. Prosperity lies in mastering the interactions of all three poles.

The definition of Enterprise Information and Communication Technology (ICT^E) adopted here is inspired by Figure 1-1 and the OEDC's definition:

> "A technology enabling knowledge transformation and transfer within the enterprise's internal structure and with its external structure and competent individual stakeholders."

By fixing the boundary of an enterprise along the dotted black line encircling the organization's internal structure in Figure 1-1, ICT^Es that are mainly relevant to individuals or external structures can find their place outside the Manufacturing Small & Medium Enterprise (MSME) discourse. ICT^Es relevant to both the external and internal structures, or for both competent individuals and internal structure, or for all three, can also find their own conceptual space. Telephones, fax machines, cell phones, email, instant messaging, desktop operating systems and word processors are ICTs which can thus be excluded from the enterprise discourse in modern society, as they are assumed to be mastered by competent individuals. In this contextualized discourse, these ICTs are positioned outside the enterprise's boundary and into the competent individual conceptual space. This subjective view is linked to which ICTs are assumed to be mastered by individuals based on regular education and common experience, and which competencies cannot be assumed to exist before the enterprise gets involved.

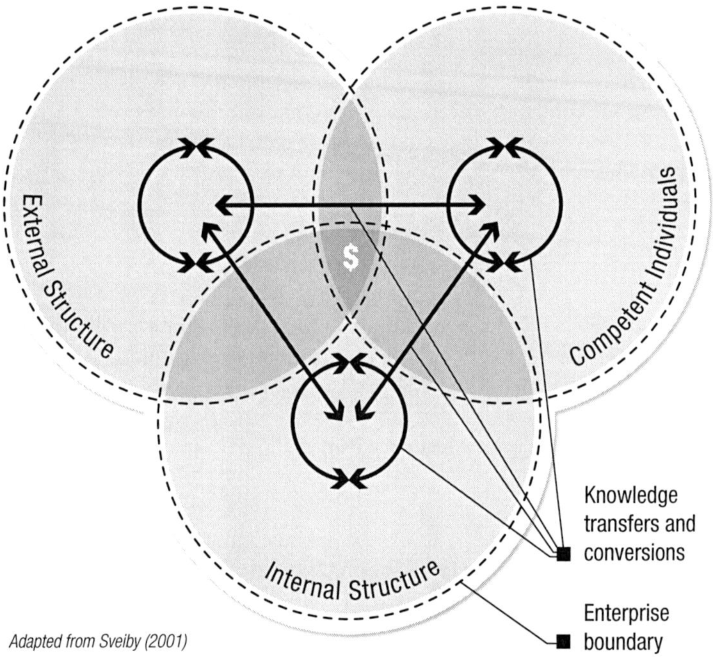

Figure 1-1 A knowledge-based view of an enterprise

ICT^{E}s that are too costly, too vast or simply impossible to access or create by individual enterprises can also be positioned outside the enterprise's boundary. Examples include the Internet's infrastructure (comprising fiber optic cables, satellites, routers and so forth), communication and information exchange standards (such as XML, PapiNet, RosettaNet), credit card networks, social networks, as well as other vast material or symbolic infrastructures. For this contextualized discourse, these are ICTs which are part of the enterprise's environment – they are part of its accessible resource toolkit and enterprises do not have to put them in place, though they may have to pay to access them.

Figure 1-1 does not imply that internal structures can be disconnected from the external world or from individuals. The enterprise's internal structure cannot exist without interacting with its external structure or the competent individuals which bring it to life. Likewise, the external structure cannot exist without firms with internal structures or without competent individuals. Competent individuals need an external structure to interact in, just as they need firms with internal structures to interact with. Figure 1-2 presents broad ICT^E types for manufacturing enterprises and positions them in four conceptual spaces along their most commonly found intent:

- Internal Structure (IS) ICT^{E}s concern knowledge transfer and transformation within an enterprise's internal structure, such as ICT that deal with improving internal product design processes;

- External Structure – Internal Structure (ESIS) ICT^{E}s concern knowledge transfer and transformation between the enterprise's internal structure and its external structure, such as ICTs that deal with value chain logistics or customer relationships;

- Competent Individuals – Internal Structure (CIIS) ICT^{E}s concern knowledge transfer and transformation between the enterprise's internal structure and its competent individuals, such as ICTs that deal with virtual team communication or employee portals;

- Competent Individuals – External Structure – Internal Structure (CIESIS) ICT^{E}s concern holistic solutions which try to deal with knowledge transfer and transformation between an enterprise's internal structure, its external structure and its competent individuals, such as all-in-one ICTs which digitize enterprises and elevate them up to best industry practices with internal, external and people processes.

Knowing which ICT^E belongs to which conceptual space in Figure 1-2 (IS, ESIS, CIIS or CEISIS) is a matter of judgment. ICT^E types evolve over time. Many ICT^{E}s offered on the market can belong to more than one type or share an acronym for marketing purposes without sharing key characteristics once put in actual use. Note that the acronyms of common ICT^E types are positioned in Figure 1-2 to illustrate the use of conceptual spaces and do not constitute an exhaustive categorization effort for these spaces.

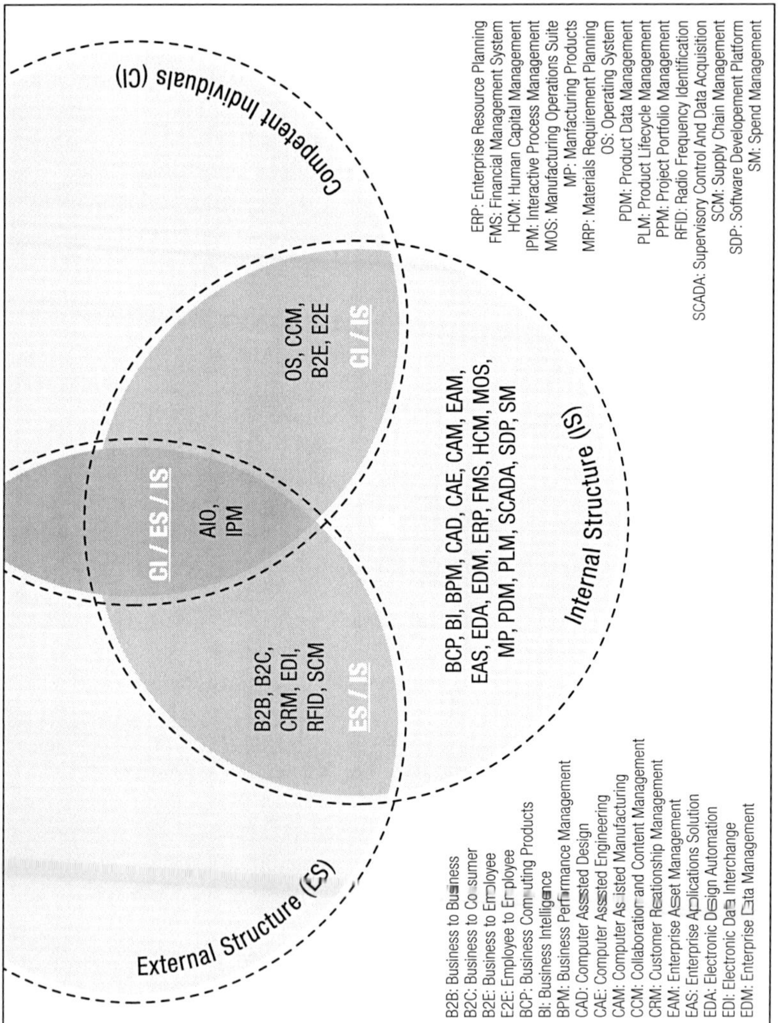

Figure 1-2 ICT conceptual positioning framework in the context of manufacturing enterprises

One could argue that all ICT^{E}s have an impact on external and internal structures, as well as competent individuals. For example, computer assisted design (CAD) software is part of the enterprise's internal structure as far as product creation and innovation are concerned, but is also part of the CIIS space when seen as a work interface between co-creating employees. Moreover, it is also part of the ESIS space when considered under the light of digital CAD files moving across the value web between various stakeholders. This type of reasoning discourages all classification attempts because it does not focus on the intended systemic effect sought by a given ICT^E. It is through such intent that classification may intelligibly take place. In this example, CAD software is primarily intended to assist in product design, and indirectly shapes work and value chain exchanges as more competent individuals start to use it. The acronym itself carries meaning which anchors CAD in the IS space of Figure 1-2.

How intended use is expressed varies, notably because ICT^E usage varies amongst manufacturing enterprises. In addition, ever more complex ICT^{E}s are grouped into solutions which can be segmented into specialized modules. For example, Enterprise Resource Planning (ERP) solutions often have invoicing or inventory management modules, but are also part of larger All-in-One (AIO) solutions and may feature modules of other AIO components that have little to do with what an ERP system commonly does. Nevertheless, strong hints of an ICT^E's intended use can be found in the label attached to it, such as *Product Lifecycle Management* (PLM) or *Supply Chain Management* (SCM). However, the definitions of these labels are evolving and sometimes contradictory between ICT makers.

2. Positioning of ICT^{E}s for manufacturing SMEs

An exhaustive catalog of ICT^{E}s aimed at Manufacturing SMEs (MSMEs) would be obsolete upon release. Aside from the huge amount of resources such a compilation would entail, one has to take into account that ICT^{E}s are created constantly and evolve over time. A critical catalog would likewise be impractical. The pros and cons of ICT^{E}s depend on each SME's business context. Choosing relevance over exhaustiveness is the only realistic option for a book discussion.

The ICT^{E}s presented here are taken from Manufacturing Business Technology's 2007 Global 100, a compilation limited to a hundred entries which favors global players with manufacturing offers. Each is positioned in one of the four conceptual spaces presented in Figure 1-2. The Global 100's five groups are preserved to show how they are distributed through these spaces. The label or acronym used to market each ICT^{E} is kept to show its developer's foreseen use, regardless of how MSMEs actually appropriate and adapt them. Each ICT^{E} was verified through website visits made during the summer of 2007 using the Global 100's URL list.

ICT^{E}s were most often grouped along industry, size, or problem solving website navigation options. ICT^{E}s in industry specific navigation were often contextualized aggregates of wider solutions, with many industries getting their own dedicated bundles. Where firm size navigation was an option, different ICT^{E} scopes were offered. SME solutions often turned out to be truncated versions of large firm solutions. Where industry or firm size navigation was not available, only ICT^{E}s with a substantial link to MSMEs were positioned. It should be understood that such substantial character was based on experience and context when dealing with all Global 100 entries. It should also be noted that some developers showcased a multitude of different products or services where others would aggregate them in comprehensive all-in-one (AIO) solutions. Offers too numerous and granular compared to similar Global 100 ICT^{E}s were positioned along their product or solution family line. Others were omitted in favor of more aggregate solutions originating from the same developer. Figure 1-3 synthesizes the Global 100 positioning exercise, presenting 29 ICT^{E} acronyms commonly found during navigation. These do not form an exhaustive list of MSME ICT^{E}s acronyms.

As shown in Figure 1-3, the IS space comprises 122 ICT^{E}s, the ESIS, 66, the CIESIS, 14 and the CIIS, 11, for a total of 213. The five Global 100 ICT families are to be found in all conceptual spaces, except CIIS, home to and focus of collaborative tools, which only features three: product innovation, computer infrastructure and business performance. The five families are grayscale-coded for easier reading, from pale to dark: product innovation is palest, followed by computer infrastructure, plant operations, logistics and value chains, and finally business performance.

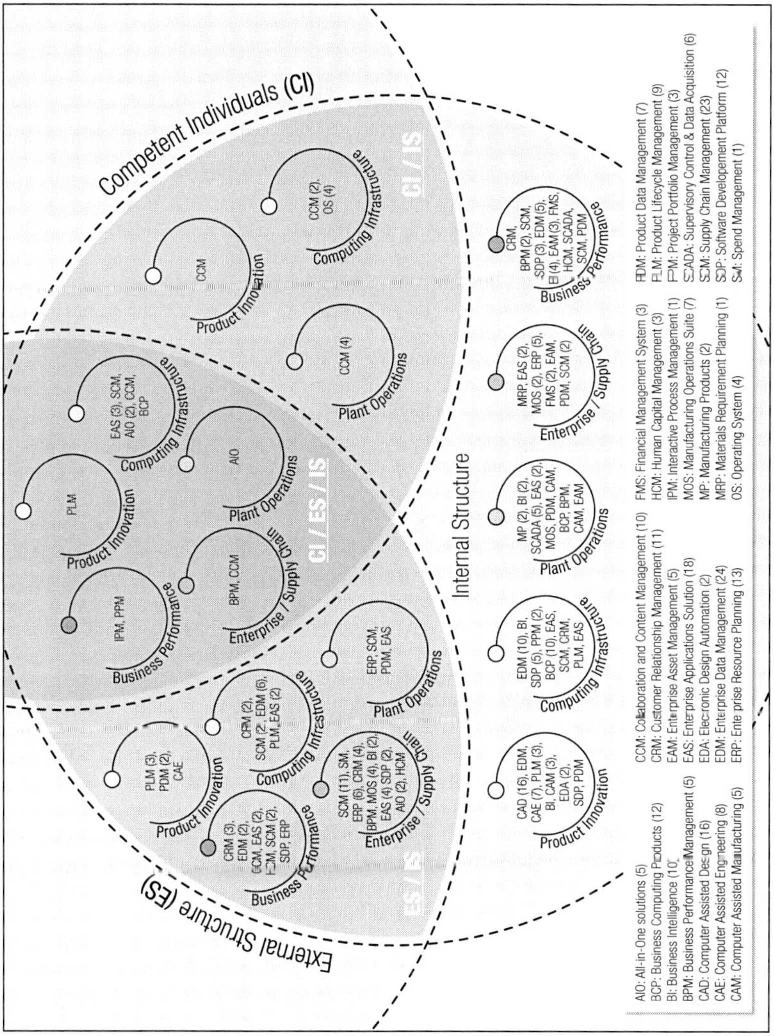

Figure 1-3 Conceptual map of Global 100 MSME ICT^{E}s

This conceptual map is much more nuanced and heterogeneous than what Figure 1-2 suggested. The five most frequent ICT^{E} types were *Enterprise Data Management* (EDM), *Enterprise Applications Solution* (EAS), SCM, CAD and ERP, though one should not forget that many solutions are modular and may thus be included under more encompassing acronyms. For example, *Customer Relationship Management* (CRM) is sometimes presented as a stand-alone ICT^{E} type, but is frequently included in AIO, EDM, SCM, EAS and ERP. This complicates any attempt to draw conclusions about the frequency of Global 100 ICT^{E} type. It may be similarly tempting to conclude that there are fewer CIIS ICT^{E}s on the market, though it is far more likely the result of a web navigation bias in favor of SMEs and manufacturing as keywords and selected options.

Figure 1-3 showcases a wide variety of MSME ICT^{E}s that mesh into one another, many being modules of more aggregate ICT^{E}s or featuring modules of other ICT^{E} types. This makes any clear-cut categorization effort suspect. The fact that new labels are constantly being created and that established ones keep evolving – as new modules are added and older ones disappear – complicates things further.

Global 100 navigation was complemented by visits to MSME ICT developer websites from Québec Chaudière-Appalaches region in the Canadian province of Quebec. A list was generated with the assistance of the administrators of Resautic.ca, a local ICT^{E} directory. The goal was to look at MSME ICT^{E}s from a locally grounded perspective, with the objective of adding complementary insight for discussion in Section 3. Out of 10 developers identified in January 2008, 9 offered one or more ICT^{E} to manufacturing SMEs: 14 ICT^{E} types, comprising 4 ERPs, 2 *Collaboration and Content Management* (CCM) as well as 8 others ; *Business Computing Products* (BCP), *Business Intelligence* (BI), CAM, *Enterprise Asset Management* (EAM), EDM, *Financial Management System* (FMS), *Human Capital Management* (HCM) and *Spend Management* (SM). All conceptual spaces were occupied by local developers, except CIESIS.

3. Emerging trends for MSME ICT^{E}s

Navigating the Global 100 revealed two major trends. First is consolidation: numerous websites featured news of fusions, acquisitions or partnerships. The result is widespread aggregation of ICT^{E}s around AIO solutions with industry-specific bundling of relevant modules. Few developers advertize a single AIO. Most propose multiple industry verticals such as aerospace, healthcare, finance and so forth, with manufacturing being one of the more commonly found options. Such bundles can be sold as a whole or in parts, as required by MSMEs. Second is web-based online ICT^E access where current bandwidth limitations make such an option viable. For example, most ERPs are operable through the web, while few CADs are. CAD interfaces need robust 3D manipulation, something which current bandwidth limitations make unavailable to most. Note that such limitations recede ceaselessly, so this trend is likely to continue until all ICT^Es are available and operable online. Such "anytime-anywhere" access also feeds mobile solutions, though more acutely limited by bandwidth, memory and processing power. *Business Intelligence* ICT^Es are the most frequent examples of mobile MSME ICT^Es.

These two trends are also found at the non-Global 100, local ICT^E developing SME scale solutions, although they find a different expression; where consolidation goes hand-in-hand with large scale AIO aggregation, local developers instead focus on compatibility and interoperability. This is likely a reflection of who owns industry standards; larger firms have the resources to fight a format war, while smaller firms hedge their bets by advertizing compatibility with a major standard solution. Choosing which global format holder to align themselves with is likely a major strategic decision for developers, since other stakeholders in the format are likely to become their main growth enablers and clients. The trend toward web deployed ICT^E is also present for local developers, which enables competition at a global scale. Interestingly, the computing infrastructure which allows ubiquitous ICT^E access worldwide is itself partly crafted from locally developed ICT^Es sold throughout the world.

These two trends feed upon a common source: the ubiquitous availability of intelligible information. Intelligibility should be understood here as a quality which enables ICT^E modularity and aggregation, while ubiquity refers to real-time, anytime, anywhere access to relevant technologies. The challenge posed to manufacturing SMEs is thus to design ubiquitous and intelligible information in a manner as, if not more, robust than the way in which they design products. This means information designed for the manufactured product, the manufacturer, as well as its entire value web, from supplier to end user.

From a high conceptual standpoint, each ICT^E developer implicitly proposes information designs through its offers, with the most holistic ones found in AIO solutions. A manufacturing SME must choose between three options: (1) to adopt a developer's information design as offered through third party ICT^E; (2) to create its own information design; or (3) to adapt a developer's design by taking what fits and by creating what it can do better than a third party. For all three options, the goal is to find what works best to enact a prosperous business design in a new economy context. In this sense, the challenge posed above can only be met if a manufacturing SME can leverage its mastery of information design to innovate not only in operational terms, but also in terms of business design.

Business design seeks to holistically represent a firm and the sum of its actions. Table 1-1, Figure 1-4 and Figure 1-5 present three conceptual frameworks meant to better enable business design and business modeling. It can be affirmed that ICT^Es should be conceptualized around such representations rather than around commercial acronyms, so that their impact on the design of a business be adequately grasped. Each of the frameworks is based on four interlaced key elements.

Simply stated, according to Table 1-1, an ICT^E can have a potential impact on the enterprise's products, its customer interface, its management infrastructure and its finances. According to Figure 1-4, an ICT^E can potentially impact on a business's customer interface, its core strategy, its strategic resources and its value network. Alternatively, according to Figure 1-5, an ICT^E can potentially impact on an enterprise's character, its creation system, its offer of products and services, and its stakeholders.

Pillar	Business Model Building Block	Description
Product	Value Proposition	Gives an overall view of a company's bundle of products and services.
Customer Interface	Target Customer	Describes the segments of customers a company wants to offer value to.
	Distribution Channel	Describes the various means the company uses to get in touch with its customers.
	Relationship	Explains the kinds of links a company establishes between itself and its different customer segments.
Infrastructure Management	Value Configuration	Describes the arrangement of activities and resources.
	Core Competency	Outlines the competencies necessary to execute the company's business model.
	Partner Network	Portrays the network of cooperative agreements with other companies necessary to efficiently offer and commercialize value.
Financial Aspects	Cost Structure	Sums up the monetary consequences of the means employed in the business model.
	Revenue Model	Describes the way a company makes money through a variety of revenue flows.

Table 1-1 Osterwalder et al.'s business model framework

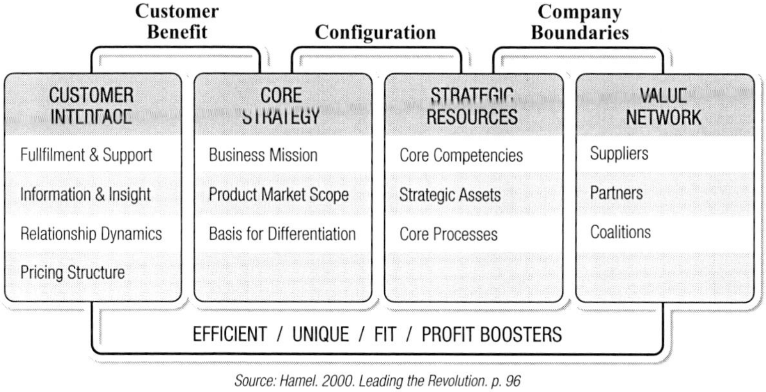

Figure 1-4 Hamel's business model framework

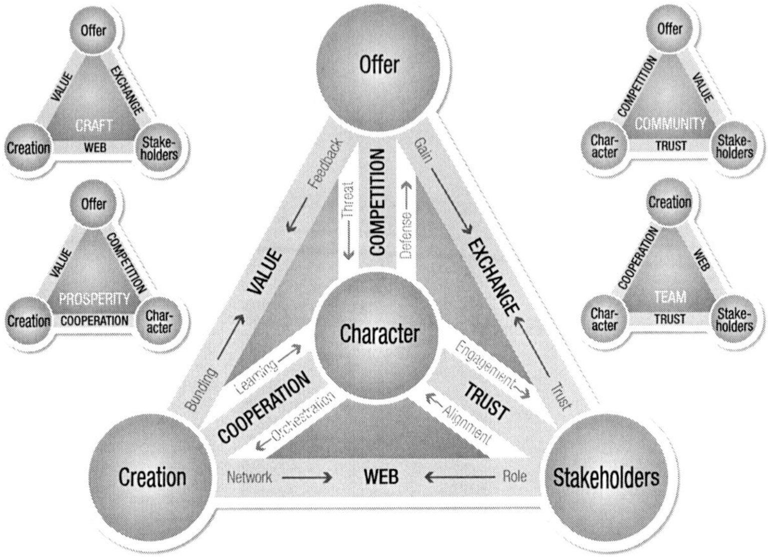

Figure 1-5 Caisse & Montreuil's Tetrahedral business design framework

Relationships between each of these three frameworks and ICT^{E}s are rich in nuances that are much more profound and subtle than is possible to highlight here. Careful study of these relationships can be most revealing for SME managers as well as for ICT^E developers, vendors and integrators.

Considering the impact of ICT^{E}s as implicit embodiments of information designs on overall business design, it appears opportune to question what it means to be a manufacturing SME. The megatrends identified above foreshadow a future where numerous SMEs would mostly be nervous systems capable of doing business with subcontractors and partners around the globe. In other words, even if the value creation web as a whole maintains the manufacturing character which is central to the manufacturing SME in this chapter, it is far from obvious that the SME which evolves into a manufacturing web orchestrator will maintain such a manufacturing character itself. It is more likely that it could be conceptualized as a piloting or orchestrating SME, with or without internal manufacturing capacity. This questioning is already pertinent at a time when numerous enterprises increasingly source their products from foreign countries.

Conclusion

ICT^{E}s are rapidly evolving. ICT^{E} categories and acronyms are ephemeral, and grand categorization schemes are subject to rapid irrelevance. There are reasons behind this, and it is more important to understand these reasons than to spend continued time and energy any dividing up the field into neat categories. The framework proposed in this chapter plays a key role in questioning such categorizing and in uncovering the broader undercurrents at work.

External structure, internal structure, competent individuals and their interrelations provide simple and elegant conceptual spaces to uncover and highlight these undercurrents. Granular, single purpose ICT^{E}s may belong to one precise conceptual space, but most are meant to be imbedded in larger ICT^{E} portfolios that link two or more conceptual spaces. This can be linked to theories of the firm which place information as the key resource that makes it possible to answer the question as to why we have firms within markets rather than markets with no firms (Conner and Prahalad 1996).

By increasingly making intelligible information accessible anytime-anywhere, ICT^{E}s provide more of that key resource to markets, firms and the competent individuals who enact them. It should come as no surprise that ICT^{E}s are broadening in scope and blurring in their intent; ICTs are expanding the realm of business possibilities for markets, firms and individuals.

The main conclusion of this chapter is that designing information and communication may turn out to be the most crucial aspect of manufacturing. How to carry out that design is a question that merits further inquiry. Some answers might be found in a closer examination of business design frameworks. Other answers might be found in crafting new frameworks and conceptual spaces. Yet other answers might be found in how design is carried out in practice, from planned and explicit attempts to chaotic trial-and-error approaches.

Numerous research opportunities are revealed through the identification of ICT^{E}s and their relationships with sustainable business survival and profitability. As mentioned by Porter (2001), it is not clear that the Internet constitutes a competitive advantage for firms, since its mastery is increasingly a market participation prerequisite and entry facilitator. Does online availability of ERPs fit in this logic? If so, many ICT^{E}s presented in this chapter are tools that could potentially be future prerequisites in the manufacturing industry, essentials for designing, building, operating and growing manufacturing SMEs. This would lead such ICT^{E}s to benefit the industry at a macroscopic level, but to have potentially no positive impact on the prosperity and business risk reduction of individual MSMEs.

CHAPTER TWO

RELATIONSHIP BETWEEN SME PERFORMANCE AND INFORMATION AND COMMUNICATION TECHNOLOGY

JEAN-FRANÇOIS ROUGÈS, DIANE POULIN, SOPHIE D'AMOURS AND BENOIT MONTREUIL

Introduction

SMEs are now recognized as having a prominent role in the economy (Griffy-Brown and Chun 2007). In a context of intensifying competition, they face many pressures, such as for productivity improvement and higher-value proposition development. In this context, information and communication technologies (ICT) are spotlighted as an emerging major driver of performance.

The literature identifies several theoretical benefits that SMEs can derive from investing in ICT (Barba-Sanchez et al. 2007; Grandon and Pearson 2004; OECD 2004; Raymond et al. 1998). A key set of these expected benefits is as follows:

- access to new and emerging markets;
- improvement of service quality;
- improved communication with customers;
- improved productivity and efficiency;
- adoption of managerial and organizational models that are more sophisticated based on decentralization and specialization;
- improved coordination with external partners which reduces transaction costs;
- lever enabling more analytical, proactive and aggressive strategic decision making.

However, many studies conclude that ICT utilization level by SMEs is still low (Asproth and Nyström 2008; Foreman-Peck et al. 2006; Martin and Milway 2007; Palvic et al. 2007; Ritchie and Brindley 2005) and that they do not derive full benefit from the ICT they do implement (Griffy-Brown and Chun 2007). SMEs do not seem entirely convinced of the advantages of investing in ICT (Martin and Milway 2007; Salmeron and Bueno 2006). Between what the theory proposes and what is observed, there is a gap that is useful to understand. Should SMEs have an interest in investing in ICT, and if so, under what conditions?

For many years, ICT research has focused on large companies. However, SMEs have different, specific characteristics. Therefore it is difficult to make inferences from the results of studies conducted in large enterprises. This raises a real need to build a conceptual framework and specific methods of intervention for SMEs (Bhagwat and Sharma 2007; Caldeira and Ward 2003; Maguire et al. 2007; Montazemi 2006). The needs for internal and external coordination of an SME are less intense (Bhagwat and Sharma 2007; Burke 2005; Raymond et al. 2005). This partly explains the fact that SME leaders are less convinced of the benefits of ICT (Martin and Milway 2007; Salmeron and Bueno 2006). SMEs also suffer from a lack of financial and human resources to manage the choice and implementation of ICT (Bhagwat and Sharma 2007; Bruque et al. 2007; Burke 2005; Caldeira and Ward 2003; Martin and Milway 2007; Montazemi 2006; Salmeron and Bueno 2006). Finally, in SMEs, the role of the leader-owner is crucial (Bhagwat and Sharma 2007; Burke 2005; Montazemi 2006; Raymond et al. 2005; Schubert and Leimstoll 2007; Winklhofer et al. 2007).

Despite growing interest on the various aspects of the use of ICT by SMEs, the literature is scarce. This has been noted by Bruque et al. (2007), Caldeira and Ward (2003) and Raymond and Bergeron (2005).

In response to this perceived gap, the goal of this chapter is to provide a literature review exploring the link between the use of ICT and performance of SMEs and to identify the factors that influence this link. The chapter is structured as follows: In the first part, we review 29 papers that explore the relationship between ICT implementation and performance of SMEs. In the second part, we study 22 papers dealing with the factors that influence this link. In the third part, we propose an integrated model of the factors which define and constrain the relationship between the use of ICT and performance in SMEs.

1. A non-systematic positive link between ICT and performance

We begin this part by highlighting the methodological difficulties encountered in studying the link between the use of ICT and the performance of SMEs, which may in part explain the discrepancies in the findings. Next, we examine reported results of ICT implementation on four key variables: income, productivity, profitability and competitive advantage establishment. We can then conclude that the existence of a link between ICT implementation and performance is not systematic.

1.1. Methodological difficulties

The study of the link between SME performance and ICT investment, implementation and usage, faces several methodological issues. First, it is particularly difficult to access reliable data, as databases on SMEs are not well developed. In addition, few SMEs have developed tools for measuring and evaluating performance indicators related to their use of the ICT they implement (Elia et al. 2007; Canadian e-Business Initiative 2004). Excluding the case studies, only seven of the 22 studies investigating the link between performance and ICT investment implementation and usage in SMEs are based on econometric evidence such as financial data and market share. These are: Esselaar et al. (2007); Ilsoon (2006); Martin and Milway (2007); OECD (2004), Raymond et al. (2005); Vemuri and Palvia (2006); Wade et al. (2004). Fifteen others use an evaluation based on the perception of respondents, which, therefore introduces bias. Furthermore, due to the difficulty of accessing SMEs, only small samples can be studied, which impairs result generalization (Levenburg 2005).

Performance measurement also generates its share of difficulties. Most studies focus on only a few key variables, as listed in Table 2-1. These do not capture all the benefits of ICT investment. Especially lacking are the intangible impacts, such as customer satisfaction increase and decision-making improvement (Santhanam and Hartono 2003; Vemuri and Palvia 2006). Several recent studies investigate new directions and have drawn the conclusion that ICT have other positive effects on performance by improving the quality of service provided to costumers (Elia et al. 2007; Lawson-Body et al. 2006), by supporting the network strategies (Asproth and Nyström 2008; Johnston et al. 2006) or by facilitating the formulation and implementation of competitive strategies (Rivard et al. 2006). As highlighted by Schlemmer and Webb (2006), the choice of dependent variables has an impact on the conclusions we draw. However, relative to ICT, the studied variables only explain part of the positive effects that have come about. Due to the limited extent of scientific knowledge, one should remain cautious about making any generic conclusion about the link between ICT investment and SME performance.

Finally, in many cases, the benefits of investment in ICT can be measured only after a period of several months or even years after implementation because of the depth of the changes that need to be carried out (Bucar et al. 2006). Accordingly, it becomes difficult to measure the benefits that can be specifically associated with the investment.

Dependent variable	Number of papers
Revenues	11
Costs	7
Productivity	5
Competitive advantage	5
Effectiveness of the manufacturing process	3
Profitability	3
Improving the quality of customer service	2
Other: cash flow, level of inventory, marketing, R & D, Employment	1 for each variable

Table 2-1 List of studied dependent variables in the reviewed literature, excluding case studies

1.2 Impact on revenues

The impact that has been most studied is revenue growth. Several econometric studies show that ICT implementation is positively correlated with higher incomes. In their study of 398 Canadian SMEs that had implemented e-business solutions, Wade et al. (2004) note that the increase in income is 3.39% on average and that there is a significant relationship between the implementation of Internet solutions and external revenue growth with both existing and new customers. The OECD (2004), studying 220 SMEs in 11 countries, and Esselaar et al. (2007) looking at 3691 SMEs from 13 African countries, arrive at the same conclusion.

However, this impact must be tempered. In the study undertaken by Raymond et al. (2005) on 108 Quebec SMEs, it is clear that the integration of e-business only explains 4% of sales growth and 5% of exports. Similarly, Wade et al. (2004) make two observations. On the one hand, the impact is low, leading to modest single-digit changes. On the other hand, the R^2 of the tests of most of their assumptions are significant, yet they are relatively small, indicating that the implementation of e-business solutions only explains a small part of the differences in performance between the companies studied. Finally, the longitudinal study by Vemuri and Palvia (2006) on 17 SMEs before and after ERP implementation shows that most companies did not experience any revenue growth.

With regard to studies based on subjective assessments,[1] several of these contend that investment in e-business solutions have an impact on sales growth (Johnston et al. 2006; Lefebvre et al. 2005; Levenburg 2005; Poon 2000; Winklhofer et al. 2007). In contrast, a study based on a sample of 400 SMEs in New Zealand by Locke (2004) showed that there is no positive correlation between investment in IT and sales or market share growth.

Several case studies have found increased revenues. For example, Sherif and Maha (2004) reported such an increase in a hotel in Egypt that had implemented a transactional website, while Muscatello et al. (2003) report the same increase in two U.S. SMEs in the manufacturing sector.

1.3 Impact on costs and productivity

Wade et al. (2004) show that there is a significant relationship between internal Internet solutions and the reduction of direct and indirect costs. The Canadian eBusiness Initiative (2004) reports a general reduction of overhead expenses, sales cost, administrative expenses, as well as a reduction in the cost of goods sold. This effect is amplified in accordance to the size of the company. Studies based on the perceptions of managers confirm these results (Elia et al. 2007; Johnston et al. 2006; Lefebvre et al. 2005; Levenburg 2005; Locke 2004; Montazemi 2006; Schubert and Leimstoll 2007).

The case study by Muscatello et al. (2003) finds a significant reduction in costs. This can be partly explained through the improvement of

---

[1] The questionnaires measure the perceptions of managers through Lickert scales.

productivity which is noted when ICT is implemented (Esselaar et al. 2007; Ilsoon 2006; Montazemi 2006). It can also be explained by an improvement of inventory management (Elia et al. 2007; Muscatello et al. 2003) and by the improved efficiency of production operations (Elia et al. 2007; Koh and Simpson 2005; Levenburg 2005).

However, this positive impact on cost reduction is not systematic. The study done by the Canadian eBusiness Initiative (2004) shows that for certain segments of small businesses, the implementation of advanced Internet solutions results in increased costs. Indeed, an increase of the cost of sold goods is reported for manufacturing SMEs having between 20 and 50 employees. A similar increase is reported for marketing and administrative costs in retail businesses having between 20 and 50 employees. Vemuri and Palvia (2006) report that for the 17 SMEs in the chemical and pharmaceutical industries of their sample firms, ERP system implementation has no impact on costs, and in some cases, it even increases costs. It should be stressed that implementation costs are very difficult to predict and are often underestimated in the project budgeting process, resulting in inflation throughout the implementation process (Muscatello et al. 2003). Finally, Johnston et al. (2006) highlight that such an effect is linked to the size of the company: the cost impact is greater in medium-sized companies than in small companies.

1.4. Impact on profitability

Due to some combination of increased revenues or lower costs, studies that focus on the study of profitability generally report a profit increase. (Foreman-Peck et al. 2006; OECD 2004; Rivard et al. 2006; Sherif and Malia 2004).

1.5. Impact on competitive advantage development

According to Schubert and Leimstoll (2007), there are two schools of thought regarding the strategic importance of ICT. The first considers that ICT has become a commodity. Due to the fact that ICT is indeed widely available on the market, ICT cannot, in and of itself, create a differentiation (Atrostic and Jarmin 2003; Carr 2003). ICT are reported to essentially have an incremental impact on the internal systems and processes of the enterprises. Their role is to support the existing strategy and not to be the core of a new strategy (Caldeira and Ward 2003; Wade et al. 2004).

In contrast, the second school of thought argues that ICT has the potential to create a competitive advantage when its implementation is accompanied by a global innovation in the business model and business processes (Koh and Simpson 2005; Maguire et al. 2007; Montazemi 2006; Rivard et al. 2006; Schubert and Leimstoll 2007).

1.6. The effect of size

When studying SMEs, size is an important criterion to consider. Studies show that in general, the bigger a company is, the more it invests in ICT (Burke 2005; Hua 2007; Tessier and Lagace 2003). The need for ICT implementation grows with the increased complexity that is related to the size of the company (Burke 2005). Medium-sized enterprises have a more sophisticated and strategic use of ICT than smaller enterprises, and they derive more benefits from ICT implementation (Bucar et al. 2006; Hua 2007; Levenburg, 2005).

The assumption that the types of investment in ICT and its impacts are different depending on the size of the enterprise can be raised, as illustrated in Figure 2-1. Medium-sized enterprises have the necessary capabilities to implement more complex ICT that leads to cost reduction through increased value chain efficiency. On the contrary, small enterprises focus on less comprehensive solutions, such as setting up websites designed to increase sales or improve productivity by automating operations which are often manual (Bowles and Wilson 2002). The study done by the Canadian eBusiness Initiative (2004) focuses on Advanced Internet Solutions (AIS) combining Internet with software, network and hardware technologies so as to improve an existing operational process or to create a new business capability. It showed the impact of AIS on the performance of SMEs varies greatly according to the size of the company. The growth of income generated by the implementation of AIS decreases with size. However, this reduction is offset by an increasing impact on cost reduction, as confirmed by the study done by Johnston et al. (2006).

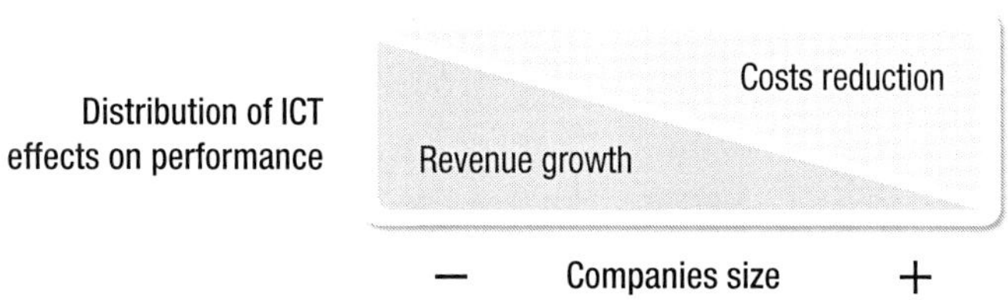

Figure 2-1 Hypothesis of the impact of investment in ICT for SMEs

Note, however, that on the contrary, some studies do not report any significant difference according to the size of the company. For example, Leimstoll and Schubert (2007) find that the size of the 989 Swiss SMEs studied has little impact on the cost, whatever the area of ICT use (internal services, purchasing, inventory management, etc.).

1.7. A link that is not systematic

Many studies conclude that there is a positive link between investment in ICT and performance. However, several studies tend to temper this assertion. In a study of twelve manufacturing SMEs, Caldeira and Ward (2003) show that the level of satisfaction with the implementation project outcomes varies considerably according to the companies. Based on a study of 395 U.S. SMEs, Levenburg (2005) shows that for the sampled organizations, having between 51 and 250 employees, there was no difference in performance between companies that have implemented e-business to more or less advanced levels. Locke (2004) examines the link between ICT and growth within 400 SMEs in New Zealand using a longitudinal approach over several years. He notes that in regard to the growth of market share and sales, there is no strong positive correlation between IT investment and growth.

The work of Olsen and Saetre (2007) goes even further by pointing out the negative effects of ICT in certain strategic circumstances. They report four case studies of SMEs in a niche market, each with between 100 and 200 employees, seeking to improve their performance through ERP implementation. They conclude that ERP is relevant to a SME which belongs to the mainstream of an industry. However, because the ERP systems impose process standards based on best practices from one area, they do not necessarily correspond to the needs of niche companies that base their competitive advantage on processes designed in-house, which allow vast offer customization. For these firms, ERP implementation can be a strategic threat.

1.8. Conclusion: a link with certain conditions

It appears, from this 29-paper review examining the impact on the performance of ICT, that the link between SME performance and ICT implementation is neither systematically positive, nor of uniform nature and impact. That is why many authors, such as Caldeira and Ward (2003), Rivard et al. (2006) as well as Hua (2007) conclude that the technology itself does not provide any competitive advantage. The ability of SMEs to benefit from ICT is influenced by a number of characteristics (Foreman-Peck et al. 2006; Grandon and Pearson 2004; Schubert and Leimstoll 2007). The next section presents a review of these characteristics.

2. Factors affecting the relationship between ICT and performance

In the reviewed literature, it appears that the link between the use of ICT and performance is neither systematic nor uniform. In an attempt to understand the reasons at the root of this phenomenon, we have studied 22 papers focusing specifically on pre-implementation conditions or success factors of ICT implementation in SMEs.

Table 2-2 presents all the variables identified in our literature review. They are grouped by topic listed in descending order of number of citations. Each topic is detailed in the following sections.

Managing the implementation of ICT	
Strategic management of the implementation project	Chien et al. (2007), Côté et al. (2005), Loh et Koh (2004), Tan et al. (2004), Tetteh and Burn (2001)
Exchanges with external experts (particularly consultants)	Chen et al. (2008), De Burca et al. (2005), Loh et Koh (2004), Martin and Matlay (2003), Yang et al. (2006)
Trade with customers and suppliers	Martin and Matlay (2003), De Burca et al. (2005), Foreman-Pecket al. (2006), Johnston et al. (2006), Ritchie and Brindley (2005)
Measuring results	Caldeira and Ward (2003), Côté et al. (2005), Loh and Koh (2004), Tan et al. (2004), Tessier and Lagace (2003)
Project planning	Chien et al. (2007), Montazemi (2006), Muscatello et al. (2003), Yang et al. (2006)
Communication with end users	Cegarra-Navarro et al. (2007), Loh and Koh (2004), Yang et al. (2006)
Existence of a sponsor in the management team	Caldeira and Ward (2003), Loh and Koh (2004), Muscatello et al. (2003)
Needs analysis	Montazemi (2006), Muscatello et al. (2003)
Gradual introduction of ICT	Barba-Sanchez et al. (2007), Johnston et al. (2006), Rivard et al. (2006)
Dynamic internal project team (composition, information sharing)	Chien et al. (2007), Loh and Koh (2004), Muscatello et al. (2003)
Knowledge management	Cegarra-Navarro et al. (2007), Johnston et al. (2006), Maguire et al. (2007)
Role of leader	Bruque et al. (2007), Winklhofer et al. (2007)
Finding the right pace of change	Barba-Sanchez et al. (2007), Caldeira and Ward (2003)
User involvement in the implementation	Chien et al. (2007), Loh and Koh (2004)
Competence / experience of project manager	Chien et al. (2007)
Change management program	Loh and Koh (2004)
Staff skills	
IT skills among employees	Hyjek and Sharp (2006), Ilsoon (2006), Jeon et al. (2006), Maguire et al. (2007), Montazemi (2006), Muscatello et al. (2003), Schubert and Leimstoll (2007) Winklhofer et al. (2007)

Staff Training	Barba-Sanchez et al. (2007), Chen et al. (2008), De Burca et al. (2005), Martin and Matlay (2003), Ritchie and Brindley (2005), Schubert and Leimstoll (2007), Yang et al. (2006)
Competence in IT project management	Eikebrokk and Olsen (2007) , Raymond et al. (1998)
Strategic management competence of IT	Barba-Sanchez et al. (2007) , Caldeira and Ward (2003)
IT skills among managers	De Burca et al. (2005), Schubert and Leimstoll (2007)
Desire of employees to work with computers	Montazemi (2006), Schubert and Leimstoll (2007)
Competencies in process reengineering	Eikebrokk and Olsen (2007)
Characteristics of technology	
Combined implantation of ICT	Lefebvre et al. (2005), Levenburg et al. (2006), Wade et al. (2004)
Sensitivity to security	OECD (2004), Schubert and Leimstoll (2007)
Compatibility and interoperability	Jeon et al. (2006), Wade et al.(2004)
Low complexity ICT	Jeon et al. (2006), Tessier and Lagace (2003)
ICT inducing reduced costs	Jeon et al. (2006), OECD (2004)
Existence of a strategic vision integrating ICT	
Develop a vision of the potential of ICT	Barba-Sanchez et al. (2007), Beckinsale et al. (2007), Caldeira and Ward (2003), Eikebrokk and Olsen (2007), Jeon et al. (2006), Raymond et al. (2005), Ritchie and Brindley (2005), Schubert and Leimstoll (2007), Winklhofer et al. (2007), Zheng et al. (2004)
Systemic Innovation	
Global innovation in business processes	Bergstrom and Stehn (2005), Côté et al. (2005), De Burca et al. (2005), Ritchie and Brindley (2005), Foreman-Peck et al. (2006), Ilsoon (2006), Muscatello et al. (2003), Vemuri and Palvia (2006)
Adjustment of HRM	Chien et al. (2007), Martin and Matlay (2003)
Culture of innovation	
Culture of innovation in the company (internal communication, empowerment of employees)	Barba-Sanchez et al. (2007), Bruque et al. (2007), Lawson-Body et al. (2006), Loh and Koh (2004), Maguire et al. (2007), Martin and Matlay (2003), Montazemi (2006), Ritchie and Brindley (2005)

Personality of the leader	
Expertise and experience of the leader	Barba-Sanchez et al. (2007), Jeon et al. (2006), Martin and Milway , Martin and Matlay (2003), Muscatello et al. (2003), Ritchie and Brindley (2005)
Strategic Alignment	
Strategic alignment	Griffry-Brown and Chun (2007), Hua (2007), Raymond and Bergeron (2008), Tsao et al. (2004)
Government Support	
Government support	Jeon et al. (2006)

Table 2-2 Factors affecting the relationship between ICT and performance in literature

2.1. The technologies themselves

The type of technology used is, in itself, a performance factor. SMEs have limited financial and human resources. They have needs that differ from those of large enterprises. The competitive advantage of a small business relies heavily on its proximity to a small number of customers. The structure of an SME tends to be more flexible, based on greater versatility. This has to be taken into account when building an ICT architecture aimed to be a performance enabler.

The introduction of low complexity solutions can limit risks and facilitate implementation in a context where competencies are limited (Jeon et al. 2006; Tessier and Lagace 2003). This also reduces implementation costs (Jeon et al. 2006; OECD 2004). To this end, the authors highlight a need for compatibility and inter-operability both internally (to link with the pre-existing systems, often customized to the operations of the SMEs) and externally (in relation with its partners and its customers) (Jeon et al. 2006; Wade et al. 2004; Winklhofer et al. 2007). Questions of safety management are also key issues. Indeed, the use of implanted ICT can be limited by concerns about security or privacy, for example in the exchange of information with supply chain partners, or in the management of access within the company (OECD 2004; Schubert and Leimstoll 2007).

The combined implementation of several technologies has a greater impact on performance than the implementation of a single solution. For example, Wade et al.'s study (2004) of 398 Canadian SMEs concludes that companies which adopt both internal and external internet solutions have double benefits when compared to those enterprises that adopt only one kind of solution. Lefebvre et al. (2005) analyzed the adoption of e-business in 192 Canadian manufacturing SMEs. They show that the intensity of profits progresses gradually as SMEs implement e-business solutions, which they attribute to a learning effect. In his study of 395 U.S. SMEs, Levenburg (2005) shows that micro-firms that had an increase in their sales and profits were supported by the use of e-management practices. Yet SMEs lack the capability and capacity needed to change everything at once. Indeed, a gradual introduction of ICT is an important factor of success as this gives time for SMEs to adapt and appropriate technologies, (Barba-Sanchez et al. 2007; Johnston et al. 2006) as well as to develop capabilities to fully adopt technology (Rivard et al. 2006).

A key issue to be resolved, and one that is poorly documented in the literature on SMEs, is whether it is preferable to use an ICT solution already available on the market or to develop proprietary solutions. Olsen and Saetre (2007) conclude that proprietary systems are relevant in certain situations, when the business model is unique and adapted to a niche. The idea that the cost of developing an in-house system is prohibitive for SMEs is widespread. Yet current development tools (web-based solutions, application generator, open source code) simplify this development and allow the interconnection of proprietary systems with existing modules. Loforte and Love (2003) and Olsen and Saetre (2007) argue that these tools enable SMEs to develop custom-made solutions that are scalable and that can be implemented gradually.

2.2. The personality of the SME leader

The decision-making process in an SME gives a central role to the leader of the enterprise. This leader brings vision, develops strategy and directs action on a daily basis. According to Schubert and Leimstoll (2007) and Winklhofer et al. (2007), unlike a large company that has in-house expertise and multiple requests from suppliers, the fate of an SME in terms of ICT depends primarily on the characteristics of its leader.

The IT competence of the leader, as well as his previous experience with IT implementation and exploitation, are success factors in ICT implementation (Barba-Sanchez et al. 2007; Jeon et al. 2006; Martin and Matlay 2003; Martin and Milway 2007; Muscatello et al. 2003; Raymond et al. 2005; Ritchie and Brindley 2005).

One determining factor is the leader's ability to have a broad vision of the impact of ICT on the development of his/her sector, which translates itself into a specific vision of its relevance to the development of a competitive advantage and the growth of the business (Beckinsale et al. 2007; Foreman-Peck et al. 2006; Zheng et al. 2004). In contrast, the literature reveals that the lack of such a vision is often an obstacle to ICT implementation in SMEs (Lefebvre et al. 2005; Zheng et al. 2004). The role that the SME leader plays throughout ICT implementation is also crucial (Bruque et al. 2007; Caldeira and Ward 2003; Winklhofer et al. 2007).

2.3. The existence of a strategic vision

For SMEs, the incentive to adopt ICT is due mainly to pressure from its environment. Most SMEs are more reactive than proactive (Grandon and Pearson 2004; Rivard et al. 2006; Winklhofer et al. 2007). They react to pressures from:

- mainly customers (Beckinsale et al. 2007; Bruque et al. 2007; Martin and Milway 2007; Poon 2000; Rivard et al. 2006; Zheng et al. 2004,
- competitors to a lesser degree (Martin and Milway 2007; Rivard et al. 2006),
- suppliers (Beckinsale et al. 2007; Poon 2000)
- network partners (Raymond et al. 2005; Zheng et al. 2004).

According to several authors, SMEs that derive the most benefit from ICT are those who have developed a strategic vision that integrates ICT (Bruque et al. 2007; Caldeira and Ward 2003; Eikebrokk and Olsen 2007; Foreman-Pecket al. 2006; Jeonet al. 2006; Ritchie and Brindley 2005). ICT appears to them as a lever that can be used to meet aggressive development targets (Bruque et al. 2007; Jeon et al. 2006; Raymond et al., 2005). This requires a detailed knowledge of the business model of the SME, its modes of operation, and its differentiation factors (Zheng et al. 2004). The study by Caldeira and Ward (2003) on twelve Portuguese SMEs shows that in the cases of greatest success, the leader is able to build a vision of ICT in his/her business, fuelled in particular by benchmarking with other SMEs. This factor is also identified by Bruque et al. (2007).

According to Raymond et al. (2005) strategic thinking about integrating ICT can take two different forms. With the strategic alignment approach, the adoption and implementation of ICT and the reconfiguration of functions and resources derive from the goals of the organization and its strategy. In contrast, with the impact approach, the new vision of the business model derives from the potential of ICT (Raymond et al. 1998).

2.4. Strategic Alignment

Successful ICT implementation consists of working in a coherent manner throughout the entire SME as a system. For example, Tsao et al. (2004) show, in their analysis of the success factors of electronic commerce adoption in Taiwanese SMEs, that the most significant factor is the integration of the Business to Business Strategy (B2B) with the marketing strategy. According to Hua (2007), four types of decisions must be coordinated: the business strategy, the ICT strategy, organizational infrastructure and technological infrastructure. This need for alignment induces a process of global innovation in the SME as a system.

2.5. Systemic Innovation

A consensus emerges in the reviewed literature: to take full advantage of ICT investments, a company needs to go beyond a "cosmetic" ICT implementation and innovate systemically. The introduction of ICT creates favorable conditions for a profound transformation of the enterprise. This consists in adapting what the company offers and its marketing, in reconfiguring its processes, in flattening its organizational structure, in strengthening its network dynamic both internally and with external partners, in adapting human resource management (skills, employment contract, behaviour), and in adopting a management style that is more democratic (Bergstrom and Stehn 2005; Côté et al. 2005; Foreman-Peck et al. 2006; Ilsoon 2006; Muscatello et al. 2003; Ritchie and Brindley 2005; Côté et al. 2005, Vemuri and Palvia 2006). Beyond the cost, the difficulties in implementing this kind of innovation are that it affects the culture of the organization, and that the SME rate of evolution is inherently slower than that of technological innovation.

By comparing the behavior of nine large companies and nineteen manufacturing SMEs in England with regard to their implementation of e-business solutions, Zheng et al. (2004) identify a particular attitude of SMEs which may partly explain their difficulties in fully exploiting ICT:

SMEs do not use e-business as a tool for global transformation of the business model, but as a series of applications that meet specific operational needs.

2.6. The management of ICT project implementation

Implementing ICT involves managing a significant and often complex project. Several project-centered success factors are identified in the literature. The management of the implementation project must be aligned with the strategic vision (Côté et al. 2005; Tan et al. 2004; Tetteh and Burn 2001). The sponsor of the project should be the leader (Bruque et al. 2007; Winklhofer et al. 2007) or a member of the management team (Muscatello et al. 2003) in which the leader has confidence (Caldeira and Ward 2003). This highlights the need to centralize the decision (Chien et al. 2007).

The selection of team members is a key success factor. Beyond the competence and experience of the project manager (Chien et al. 2007), a positive, dynamic, mutual assistance and exchange of information, based on solidarity, is necessary within the team (Raymond et al. 1998; Muscatello et al. 2003; Chien et al. 2007). The management of the project requires the mastering of specific skills. A lack of in-house expertise may be offset by the support of IT suppliers, the use of consultants, or benchmarking (Caldeira and Ward 2003; Chen et al. 2008; De Burca et al. 2005; Martin and Matlay 2003; Montazemi 2006; Yang et al. 2006).

The first step, which aims at defining the needs and the objectives that will enable an informed choice of solutions, is decisive to ultimate success (Caldeira and Ward 2003; Muscatello et al. 2003). However, the SMEs, due to lack of time and skills, do not always devote the necessary effort early on. In a comparative study, Montazemi (2006) shows that U.S. manufacturing SMEs develop further their analysis phase and their long-term planning than their Canadian counterparts do. This, in turn, creates the foundations for better management of IT projects, including better integration of users, hence creating a better climate.

The second stage involves detailed planning of the project (Montazemi 2006; Muscatello et al. 2003; Yang et al. 2006). ICT implementation is a complex process which involves technical, organizational, operational and human dimensions. In a study of 300 Canadian SMEs, Hyjek and Sharp (2006) show that a key frustration concerning ICT implementation in businesses with fewer than 100 employees is the growth, over time, of implementation costs that were not adequately anticipated. Note that as well as defects in planning, lack of skills contributes to this phenomenon.

In the implementation process, user information (Cegarra-Navarro et al. 2007; Yang et al. 2006) and user involvement (Bruque et al. 2007; Caldeira and Ward 2003; Chien et al. 2007) are indispensable. In a context of systemic innovation, involvement of customers, suppliers and partners is also necessary (Foreman-Peck et al. 2006; Martin and Matlay 2003, Ritchie and Brindley 2005). Due to interactions with senior management, solution vendors, consultants, users, partners, or even within the project team, and because of the learning curve involved in the process, ICT implementation is increasingly becoming a knowledge management process (Cegarra-Navarro et al. 2007; Johnston et al. 2006; Maguire et al. 2007).

Several authors stress the importance of finding the right pace of change, taking into account the strategic vision and the company's ability to change. The latter is particularly influenced by the competency available and the culture of the company (Caldeira and Ward 2003). Barba-Sanchez et al. (2007) conclude that the change must be implemented gradually. Finally, Tessier and Lagace (2003) argue that the HR policy is a central element to overall success as it can be used to cope with resistance and to secure participation and commitment.

Finally, the development of measurement tools to measure progress is rare (Caldeira and Ward 2003; Côté et al. 2005; Tan et al. 2004; Tessier and Lagace 2003).

2.7. Internal skills

The level of expertise available in-house has a significant effect on the impact technology will have (Barba-Sanchez et al. 2007; Bruque et al. 2007; De Burca et al. 2005; Jeon et al. 2006; Maguire et al. 2007; Montazemi 2006; Muscatello et al. 2003; Schubert and Leimstoll 2007; Tessier and Lagace 2003; Winklhofer et al. 2007).

At the first level, any ICT implementation must be accompanied by significant training efforts in order to develop technical know-how (Barba-Sanchez et al. 2007; Raymond et al. 2005). Bruque et al. (2007) showed in a study of 15 SMEs from Andalusia that one success factor is the rapid and effective use of technology enabled by intensive training efforts.

Using a waterfall-like training approach, giving, in some cases, the role of trainer to younger staff more familiar with ICT, the most successful enterprises have exceeded the mere technical training to create an effect of socialization in their organizational development.

The second level is operational competence in the management of IT projects, both in terms of ability to make the right choices and in terms of managing the implementation and the changes it induces (Eikebrokk and Olsen 2007; Raymond et al. 1998).

The third level concerns competence in the strategic management of IT. According to Caldeira and Ward (2003) and Eikebrokk and Olsen (2007), it determines the long-term success of an SME in its use of ICT. In their study of 12 Portuguese manufacturing SMEs, Barba-Sanchez et al. (2007) show that the least successful companies in adopting and using ICT attached more importance to the quality of the solutions they acquired, rather than to the development of in-house IT skills. The best performing enterprises have gone beyond the simple technical training and created communities contributing to the organizational development of the enterprise. The most successful tried to develop continuous learning dynamics in order to enable their team to better manage their IT according to their business challenges.

SMEs face two major difficulties in developing in-house IT expertise. The first is in identifying the profile of the IT experts they need. This requires a clear understanding of the business's challenges in terms of ICT. The second is to attract these experts and retain them by using working conditions and career prospects that an SME has to offer (Caldeira and Ward 2003). ICT alone does not provide a competitive advantage. However, the internal development of ICT expertise contributes to the creation of a sustainable competitive advantage because it is difficult to replicate (Caldeira and Ward 2003; Rivard et al. 2006).

2.8. Culture

The culture of the company can be an inhibitor or a facilitator of the ability of SMEs to benefit from their ICT investment (Barba-Sanchez et al. 2007; Bruque et al. 2007). The first dimension concerns how sensitive the organizational culture is to technology. Montazemi (2006) shows that employees' attitude towards IT is more positive in the United States than it is in Canada, which helps to generate the greater impact coming from the use of IT in U.S. companies. A more educated (Montazemi 2006) or younger (Bruque et al. 2007) workforce has a more developed IT culture. Thus, Muscatello et al. (2003) show in their study of two SMEs that the company from the high-tech sector has a culture that is more prone to ICT when compared to the company from the textile industry.

In the context of systemic transformation, the second dimension is a company's ability to develop a culture of innovation that values continuous improvement, mutual exchange, open discussion about problems and concerns, and an ability to share knowledge (Barba-Sanchez et al. 2007; Bruque et al. 2007, Lawson-Body et al. 2006; Maguire et al. 2007; Martin and Matlay 2003; Montazemi 2006; Ritchie and Brindley 2005). The empowerment of employees is necessary, for example, to maximize the use of a Customer Relationship Management tool (CRM) by allowing staff to react directly so as to satisfy customers (Lawson-Body et al. 2006). In particular, this can lead to a questioning of the practices of human resource management (Chien et al. 2007; Jeon et al. 2006).

3. An integrated model

After the literature review, we next propose an analytical framework integrating the link between ICT implementation and SME performance. The model (see Figure 2-2) has three types of elements which, according to the literature, serve to determine this relationship: the system of variables detailed in Part 2, the relationship between these variables that cause a systemic innovation, and finally the time variable.

Our literature review identifies a system of six variables that influence the link between ICT use and performance. In the model, they are organized around three poles borrowed from the work of Goshal and Bartlett (1997): project, processes and people.

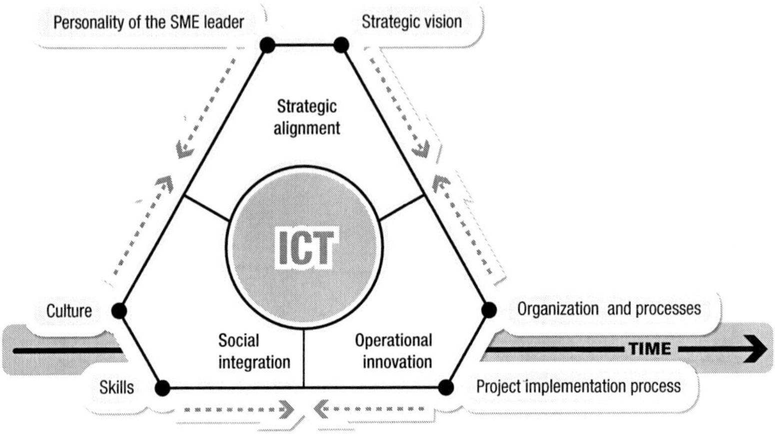

Figure 2-2 Success factors of ICT implementation in an SME

An observation emerges from the literature: SMEs that take advantage of ICT are those who use it at a strategic level by exploiting their potential for transformation. The ability of SMEs to develop a vision of the impact of ICT in their business, and their potential in transforming their business model, is a significant factor.

However, the project of an SME -- its vision, strategy, and values -- are strongly influenced by the leader. The strategy pursued is often influenced by the life goals of the leader. His influence in strategic decision making is crucial. The competence and experience of leadership in ICT will have a major impact on the vision, strategies and decisions made by the SMEs concerning ICT. The personality of the leader is a critical variable with regard to the integration of ICT in the project of the company. Therefore the first pole of the integrated model, the project, brings together the strategic vision and the personality of the leader.

The second pole deals with processes, mode of operation and the structure of the company. Some are more suited to ICT than others. For example, a lean manufacturing operation can take full advantage of an MRP. Close collaboration between sales, marketing and production permits the exploitation of the information provided by a CRM system. In addition, the management of the implementation process of ICT is in itself a variable of success. The quality of the project team, its modes of interaction with users, consultants and vendors, as well as the rigor of project management implementation, are identified as factors that influence the quality of implementation and therefore the ability to take better advantage of technology.

Finally, the impact of ICT is influenced by human factors: the skills available and the organizational culture. Three types of skills are required. Technical skills relate to the ability of employees to use the software. It is also necessary to access specific skills for the operational management of the implementation project. Finally, skills concerning the strategic management of ICT enable the development of a long term strategic vision integrating ICT. It also enables the strategic management of ICT. An organizational culture oriented towards innovation that promotes information sharing and permanent rethinking, as well as empowerment, is also identified as a factor for success.

According to the literature, ICT implementation needs a component of systemic innovation to generate performance. In our model, this systemic innovation is divided into three interrelated dynamics: strategic alignment, operational innovation, and social integration.

Business strategy and ICT strategy mutually influence each other to produce strategic alignment. On the one hand, an SME chooses ICTs because they enable the SME to achieve its strategic objectives. On the other hand, the strategy is changing because ICT offers new possibilities. Depending on the context, these two dynamics can be more or less influenced by each other. In some cases, ICTs are seen as enablers of the corporate strategy, their influence on the strategy is very small. In other cases, the business strategy is strongly influenced by the potential of ICT. In an SME, the personality of the leader will have a major influence on this balance. The rest of the organizational system (processes, modes of operation, structure, process of implementation of ICT, skills and culture) will also be affected and should evolve in order to support the strategy and its use of ICT.

Process, modes of operation, organization and ICT are also highly interdependent. An ICT is chosen because it is consistent with the processes and modes of operation of an SME and because it will help to improve them. The implementation process also depends on the chosen ICT. Therefore, ICTs are at the heart of a dynamic operational innovation that will influence skills, culture, and strategy.

Finally, the success of ICT depends on the ability of human

integration. The internal competencies in terms of ICT affect the ability to take advantage of the ICT implemented. Some ICTs are more suited than others to certain cultures. This human integration also impacts the processes and modes of operation to be set up, as well as the strategic choices.

This triple dynamic of strategic alignment, operational innovation and social integration occurs over time. Furthermore, the benefits of implementing a strategic ICT cannot be measured in the short term. Through a systemic innovation, radical changes are to be carried out. The effects of a successful use of ICT are synergistic and lead the company into a spiral of increasing performance. The literature shows that it takes around 18 months of effort to reap the benefits of an ICT implementation.

Conclusion

A review of 29 articles examining the impact of ICT on the performance of SMEs and 22 articles dealing with the conditions of success shows that the link between ICT and performance is positive, but neither systematic nor linear. Consequently, investing in an ICT does not guarantee performance and may constitute a strategic risk.

Based on the literature, we propose a model for analyzing the relationship between implementation of an ICT and performance in an SME. It is composed of six variables: the personality of the leader, the strategic vision, the organization and processes, the management process of implementation, skills and culture. Three dynamics between these six variables fuel a systemic innovation that determines the ability to generate performance through the implementation of ICT: strategic alignment, operational innovation and social integration. This evolution occurs over time. Thus, the impact of ICT on performance can only be seen over time.

This model represents a significant theoretical contribution to the extent that it is the first, to the best of our knowledge, to propose a framework for the systemic analysis of the factors influencing the relationship between ICT and performance. As such, it provides a conceptual framework to better understand and predict the ability of SMEs to take advantage of ICT implementation.

Note

The articles selected for this literature review came from several sources. Initially, they were found through a research conducted on the EBSCO and ABI/Inform Global databases over the last 10 years, using the following keywords: SME + ERP, SME + Information and Communication Technology (ICT), SME + CRM, SME + SCM. Others were drawn from the reference list of these articles. Three studies of Canadian organizations, the country of origin of the authors, were also consulted. Here is a breakdown of the articles selected for this literature review: There are 29 papers studying the impact on performance; among these, seven rely on econometric data, fifteen rely on perceptual evaluations, and seven rely on case studies. Twenty-two papers study the conditions for successful implementation. Finally, three are literature reviews.

CHAPTER THREE

THE ALIGNMENT OF IT IN SMES AND ITS CONTRIBUTION TO PERFORMANCE: RESEARCH DIRECTIONS

JEAN-FRANÇOIS ROUGÈS, DIANE POULIN, FRANÇOIS BERGERON AND YAN CIMON

Introduction

Managing the strategic alignment of information and communication technologies (ICT) with business strategy has long been a major concern of business leaders (Benbya and McKelvey 2006; Chen et al. 2008; Hirschheim and Sabherwal 210001; Newkirk et al. 2008; Raymond and Bergeron 2008; Reich and Benbasat 2000; Tallon 2008). It is also a topic that has been examined a great deal by researchers (Chan and Reich 2007). Nevertheless, theoretical and methodological problems remain (Tallon 2008). From an empirical point of view, ambiguities arise in regard to the impact of alignment on performance (Byrd et al. 2006). Several authors have even questioned whether, in the context of accelerated change, alignment is possible, or even desirable (Chan and Reich 2007). Watson (2007) raises this issue directly in an article entitled "Is strategic alignment still a priority?".

Given these differences, it is interesting to review the literature that has been written thus far. This chapter is structured as follows. In the first part, the concept of alignment is defined. In a second part, we consider methodological approaches to measure alignment. In a third part, we present the results of studies on the relationship between IT strategic alignment and performance, and we highlight the paradoxes that emerge. We see that the link is neither universal nor uniform. In a fourth section, we explain the factors involved in the building of alignment, and in a fifth part, the research challenges relating to IT strategic alignment are discussed. Finally, suggestions are made concerning the research directions that could be undertaken to meet these challenges.

1. Definition of alignment

According to the contingency theory that has prevailed in the literature on organizational design and performance, no strategy is universally superior (Van de Ven and Drazin 1985). In this perspective, both the creation of a competitive advantage and the performance of an organization are directly related to the alignment of the organization's strategy and structure with its environment (Bergeron et al. 2004; Bergeron et al. 2001; Venkatraman 1989). Given the importance that IT now has in the functioning of existing organizations, its alignment with the structure and strategy of the organization, as well as the external environment, has become a major issue (Newkirk et al. 2008). A synthesis of the definitions of IT alignment described in the literature highlights three dimensions (see Table 3-1).

The strategic alignment of IT
1. Is the level of consistency between IT strategy and business strategy in regards to its mission, its objectives and its action plans. 2. Translates at an operational level by an alignment of infrastructures and resources. 3. Is a process that is in constant adjustment.

Table 3-1 A definition of the concept of strategic alignment of IT

1.1 The domains of alignment

There are four domains, taken into consideration in the main models that explore IT alignment[1]: the business strategy, the IT strategy, the organizational structure and the IT structure. We will see that a systemic approach broadens the scope of the areas studied.

The axis of IT alignment that appears essential in the literature, and also the one that is the most studied, is the consistency between IT strategy

[1] The SAM model (Strategic Alignment Model) from Henderson and Venkatraman (1993) is the most used. However, other models have been developed. See: MIT (Chan and Reich, 2007), the Baets (1992) model, or the Sabherwal et al. (2001) model.

and business strategy with regard to the mission, objectives and action plans (Chan et al. 2006; Reich and Benbasat 2000).

1.2 The deductive vision: Business strategy leads IT strategy

One approach considers the business strategy as being the point of departure. IT strategy then serves to support business strategy by providing the resources and infrastructure needed to create and sustain a competitive advantage (Bergeron et al. 2004; Chan et al. 2006; Croteau et al. 2007). Henderson and Venkatraman (1993) speak of "strategic implementation."

1.3 The interdependence

Another approach, by contrast, sees the two strategies as interdependent (Chan and Reich 2007; Henderson and Venkatraman 1991; Newkirk et al. 2008; Peppard and Breu 2003). In this perspective, an innovative use of IT could lead to a new business strategy which, in turn, might influence the actual use of IT, and so on. This is another way for the alignment process to lead to higher organizational performance. (Bergeron and Raymond 1995; Croteau and Bergeron 2001; Hirschheim and Sabherwal 2001) (see Table 3-2).

At an operational level, strategic alignment is reflected in an alignment of IT and organizational infrastructure (Chan and Reich 2007) with competencies (Raymond and Bergeron 2008).

Finally, alignment is not an end *per se* (i.e., a unique outcome), but rather an ongoing process that continuously adjusts to changes in both the environment and strategy (Benbya and McKelvey 2006; Croteau et al. 2007; Hirschheim and Sabherwal 2001; Raymond and Bergeron 2008; Peppard and Breu 2003).

Traditional view: IT strategy operationalizes business strategy	
Chan et al. (2006, p. 27)	"IS strategic alignment is defined as the degree to which the mission, objectives and plans contained in the business strategy are shared and supported by the IS strategy"
Croteau et al. (2007, p.147)	"The alignment of IT is a continuous and dynamic process aiming at providing organizations with technological solutions enabling them to achieve their performance goals as dictated by their business strategy"
Renewed vision: IT strategy and business strategy to interact	
Newkirk et al. (2008, p. 201)	"Strategic IS alignment is the correspondence between the IS plan and the business plan such that the content of the business plan reflects the content of the IS plan, and the content of the IS plan reflects the content of the business plan"

Table 3-2 Definitions of IT strategic alignment

2. The methodological approaches used to measure alignment

2.1. The selection approach

The "Darwinian" theory of natural selection assumes that in the long term, only those organizations tailored to their environment will survive. The environment selects organizations that are aligned. This approach uses the method of matching to study how pairs of variables are interrelated in order to identify the situations of alignment (Chan and Huff 1993). For example, Levy et al. (2001) find that, depending on the strategy (i.e., cost-based or value-added-based) and the level of customer dependency (i.e., few or many customers), the technology implemented by SMEs are different. Therefore, they conclude that there is an alignment between the ICT implemented, the strategy pursued, and the level of customer dependency.

Another example from Raymond et al. (1995) shows that levels of IT sophistication (i.e., diversity and quality of IT implemented, mechanisms for managing the IT function) and the structural sophistication of SMEs in their sample (i.e., formalization, professionalization, complexity) are clearly linked. Next, the authors test the relationship between IT sophistication and structural sophistication among the most and least efficient enterprises of the sample. They show that a greater alignment between the two variables is found in the most efficient enterprises. They therefore conclude that when an IT function and IT practices are managed with greater sophistication, and are within the appropriate organizational structure, the better the company's performance.

2.2. The interaction approach

The second approach is based on interaction (Drazin and Van de Ven 1985; Van de Ven and Drazin 1985). This approach directly addresses the issue of performance (Chan and Huff 1993). The aim is to explain variations in a third variable (for example, the organizational performance) related to the interaction between two variables; the bivariate interaction. Two methods can be used to test pairs of variables: moderation and mediation (Venkatraman 1989). Moderation measures how the interaction between two variables has an impact on performance. For example, Bergeron et al. (2001) found that a better alignment between structure and IT strategic management has an impact on performance. Mediation allows for the study of a variable's direct effect on a dependant variable such as performance. Moderation allows for the study of a variable's indirect effect on the same dependant variable. For example, Bergeron et al. (2001) observed that the strategic orientation has a direct and indirect impact on performance through IT strategic management.

The interaction approach is interesting for several reasons. It can be used to test the impact of the alignment of pairs of variables on performance. Furthermore, it allows us to distinguish, among a series of pairs of variables, which pairs have the greatest impact on performance (Drazin and Van de Ven 1985). Advanced statistical methods such as partial least squares can be used to test groups of pairs of variables.

2.3. The systemic approach

In order to overcome the limitations of the interaction approach, the systemic approach was developed. This approach adopts a holistic perspective. The models include a system of variables, and thus, can take into account their interactions. According to Drazin and Van de Ven (1985), this approach allows the development of a richer understanding of the phenomenon of alignment.

Three types of alignment can be studied: covariation, profile deviation and gestalt (Venkatraman 1989). Covariation measures the impact of the coalignment of several interrelated variables on performance, such as the cross-sharing of knowledge, the history of success, size, and environmental uncertainty (Chan et al. 2006). Profile deviation measures the gap with an ideal profile identified (Bergeron et al. 2004; Raymond and Bergeron 2008), by analyzing the practices of the best enterprises in the sample or through a Delphi method (Tallon 2008). Finally, one last approach aims at finding frequently recurring clusters of attributes in a system of variables. These patterns are called gestalts (Kefi and Kalika 2005; Venkatraman 1989). These configurations are different types of alignment. Next, it is possible to compare their respective impact on performance. For example, Bergeron et al. (2001) found that four patterns of alignment, more or less efficient, emerge around four variables: strategic orientation, structural complexity, IT strategic management and environmental uncertainty.

2.4. Complementary approaches

The three approaches are not exclusive but provide different sources of information that may be useful to compare and analyze. Several approaches could be used in the same study in order to compare the results (Bergeron et al. 2001; Chan and Reich 2007; Drazin and Van de Ven 1985; Van de Ven and Drazin 1985; Venkatraman 1989) underlining the importance for the researchers to identify the type or alignment they want to test before they begin data-collection. Bergeron et al. (2001) tested six types of alignment and they found that different approaches confirm the impact of different pairs of variables on performance: strategy-technology for mediation and covariation approaches, structure-technology for moderation and matching approaches. As for profile deviation and gestalt approaches, these configurations tend to generate higher performance than others. They conclude that the choice of the strategic alignment model is dependent upon the theoretical stance.

3. The link between alignment and performance

There are only a small number of empirical studies that have operationalized alignment and demonstrated its effect on organizational performance (Bergeron et al. 2004). Therefore, Chan and Reich (2007), in their extensive literature review, cite the few studies found on this subject. The methodological difficulty is probably a factor which explains this scarcity (Tallon 2008). There are even fewer studies concerning SMEs. In this section, we present the results of eleven articles which study the impact of alignment on the performance of SMEs. We will first discuss the studies on bivariate interactions, and then multivariate analysis. We then conclude by noting that the link is neither universal nor uniform.

3.1. The results of studies on bivariate interactions

Table 3-3 presents the results of eleven empirical studies examining the impact of IT alignment on performance in SMEs. Most empirical studies on large enterprises or SMEs focus on bivariate analysis. The pair most frequently studied is IT strategy - business strategy (Bergeron et al. 2004).

These studies find a significant and positive impact on performance. Since the Palmer and Markus's study (2000) seems to be the only that finds no relationship with performance, it is therefore possible to conclude that an optimal alignment between the IT strategy and the business strategy tends to generate superior performance.

Alignment domains	**Authors**	**Form of fit**	**Relationship between alignment and performance**
Bivariate interaction			
Business strategy, IT strategy	Bergeron and Raymond (1995)	Mediation, moderation	Positive impact
Structural sophistication, IT sophistication	Raymond et al. (2005)	Matching, moderation	Positive impact
Business strategy, IT strategy	Teo and King (1996)	Mediation	Positive impact
Business strategy, IT strategy	Chan et al. (1997)	Matching, moderation	Positive impact
Business strategy, IT strategy	Palmer and Markus (2000)	Profile deviation	No relationship
Strategic IT management; structure	Bergeron et al. (2001)	Moderation, matching	Positive impact
Environmental uncertainty, strategic orientation	Bergeron et al. (2001)	Moderation	No relationship
Requirements for accounting information, capacity of accounting systems	Ismail and King (2006)	Matching	Positive impact
E-business capabilities, business	Raymond and Bergeron (2008)	Profile deviation	Positive impact, vary in the relation to the strategic orientation (impact on profitability for defenders

			and on productivity for prospectors)
Multivariate interaction			
Business strategy, business structure, IT strategy, IT structure	Bergeron et al. (2004)	Covariation	Generally positive, but particularities for some groups
Markets, products, networks, advanced manufacturing technologies	Raymond and Croteau (2006)	Gestalt	Positive impact

Table 3-3 Summary of studies between alignment and performance

3.2. Multivariate studies

The bivariate analysis is limited since it assumes that everything can be broken down into constitutive elements (i.e., pairs) that can be studied independently (Drazin and Van de Ven 1985). A holistic approach provides a better explanation as it takes into account the effects of interrelationships between variables. In recent years, researchers test multivariate models in a more systemic perspective (Bergeron et al. 2004; Raymond and Croteau 2006).

These studies highlight that there are several configurations of alignment that are more or less proficient. In configurations where there is a conflict in the coalignment between domains, a negative impact on performance is measured (Bergeron et al. 2004). Thus, a portrait of the most successful SMEs, the so-called "world class" SMEs, seems to emerge from these studies (Raymond and Croteau 2006). They have a robust strategic approach (i.e., the SME takes the time to analyze its performance in order to predict and anticipate the future), a complex organizational structure (i.e., highly formalized, specialized and differentiated), a strategic use of cutting edge IT and a highly structured IT function (Bergeron et al. 2004). They are more aggressive regarding product innovation and market development. They have a growth strategy based on networking and partnering. They also have a higher level of integration of advanced production technologies and have developed a greater capacity to integrate technology, which allows them to maintain their competitive advantage (Raymond and Croteau 2006).

However, the alignment itself is not a sufficient condition for higher performance. In order for the coalignment to have an impact on performance, it is necessary for each domain to have reached a certain level. Yet, a particularly strong domain can compensate for the lack of alignment and generate more performance. (Bergeron et al. (2004) show that an IT staff of a group of SMEs who were highly motivated to identify and implement profitable IT, managed to generate a level of performance equivalent to that of a group of SMEs who had the highest level of coalignment. This suggests that factors of social dynamics can compensate for a lack of coalignment.

3.3. An impact neither universal, nor uniform

Several studies conclude that IT strategic alignment has an impact on performance. However, this impact is not universal (Chan and Reich 2007). In recent years, models have been refined and allow us to go beyond general statements. By incorporating the strategy pursued into models (Raymond and Bergeron, 2008), or by adopting the multivariate approach (Bergeron et al. 2004), the findings show more contrast than previously thought in regard to the universality of the impact (i.e., observed for all enterprises) and its uniformity (i.e., the same effect on performance).

Regarding the universality of the impact of alignment on performance, Tallon (2008) emphasizes in his literature review that out of the six studies that take into account the difference between strategies, only two of them conclude that better alignment generates better performance for all types of strategies. In particular, many studies on large companies show that the defenders do not take advantage of their alignment (Sabherwal and Chan et al. 2001; Chan et al. 2006; Tallon 2008).

The study by Raymond and Bergeron (2008) of 107 Canadian SMEs illustrates the non-uniformity of the impact of alignment on performance. When considering the entire sample, the alignment between the capabilities of e-business and business strategy has an impact on the productivity and profitability of a business (but not on their growth). More specifically, according to the strategies adopted by SMEs, it appears that the impact of alignment on performance is not uniform and reveals several paradoxes. For defenders, the impact of alignment is on growth and profitability, while we would expect an impact on productivity (which is the focus of this strategy). For analysts, the impact is on growth and profitability. For prospectors, the impact is on productivity (and not on growth, although this strategy emphasizes market share and innovative offer development). To explain these paradoxes, the authors put forward two hypotheses. First, defenders may already have a high level of productivity before the introduction of e-business solutions. Next, prospectors may depend on large key customers who, in turn, may remain unresponsive to e-business solutions. Different impacts are observed depending upon the strategic orientation of the firms.

3. 4. Emerging trends: understanding the building of alignment

The relationship between alignment and performance is neither universal nor uniform. Specific situations that are indeed paradoxical are found. This underscores the need to better understand how the alignment is built. Several methodological approaches have been developed to do so. We present some of these approaches in this section: analysis of micro-alignment (Tallon 2008), the longitudinal analysis (Chen et al. 2008; Croteau et al. 2007; Hirschheim and Sabherwal 2001), and the co-evolution approaches (Benbya and McKelvey 2006; Breu and Peppard 2003).

3.4.1. A micro approach: process alignment

Much research on alignment is based on types of strategies[2] and does not take into account how companies implement these strategies. However, identical strategies can be implemented through different processes and activities. From this perspective, the goal of alignment is not to achieve an undifferentiated alignment of all processes. Rather, the goal is to seek the type of micro-alignment that is relevant, taking into account the mix of processes and key activities needed to carry out the chosen strategy. If a tight alignment is essential for key processes, a loose alignment, or even a non-alignment of the secondary processes has virtually no impact on performance. According to the resource-based view theory, it is the unique configuration of processes, activities and competencies that creates a sustainable competitive advantage. In order to understand the impact of alignment on performance, and to explain the differences and paradoxes found, it is thus necessary to go beyond an analysis of the strategic types and to study the implementation process (Tallon 2008).

---

[2] From a methodological point of view this means the use of typologies such as of Miles and Snow, and Porter.

This new theoretical framework is tested in Tallon's (2008) pioneer study performed on a sample of large enterprises. Drawing on the discipline of value developed by Treacy and Wiersema (1997), the author develops a theoretical profile that links the type of strategy with key processes. On the one hand, the study concludes that a greater alignment between the key processes and the disciplines of value generates performance for the firms pursuing strategies of customer intimacy and product leadership. However, for those pursuing cost-based strategies, there is no link between alignment and performance. This study is thus coherent with the literature that shows the difficulties faced by the defenders in taking advantage of the alignment. On the other hand, along with these assumptions, the alignment of secondary processes has a lower impact. Finally, the use of IT creates value when used in the key processes.

This micro approach, with regard to processes, thus offers an explanation for the "paradox of defenders" who adopts a strategy of operational excellence. It appears that a greater alignment in the key processes of this strategy[3] has no positive impact on performance. This does not mean that this alignment is not important for the discipline of value, but that it does not allow enterprises to differentiate themselves. In other words, operational excellence is a must for all strategies. An enterprise that is not operationally reliable (with respect to the quality of its products, the reliability of its deadlines, etc.) cannot exist on the market regardless of its promise to customers. The Defenders minimize the alignment of three secondary processes in their discipline of value (i.e., improvement of their offer, sales support and marketing, and customer relationships), without creating an alignment of their core processes that is superior to that of other strategies (i.e., focus on the relationship between suppliers and operations). Thus, Tallon (2008) concludes that the defender strategy is a survival strategy rather than a differentiation strategy.

The micro approach allows us to understand alignment with a greater level of detail. However, we are not aware of any study that applies it to the context of SMEs. This is, therefore, a promising research perspective.

---

[3] In this case two processes: (1) relationships with suppliers, (2) production and operations

3.4.2. The longitudinal approach

The definition of alignment recognizes that it is a continuous process and not a result (Croteau et al. 2007; Hirschheim and Sabherwal 2001; Raymond and Bergeron 2008). Maintaining alignment over time can be difficult in a context where there are rapid environmental and technological changes. Many authors consider that a longitudinal approach is needed in order to understand the building of alignment and its impact on performance (Bergeron et al. 2004; Bergeron and Raymond 2008; Chan and Reich 2007). Yet, research adopting this approach is still underdeveloped (Chen et al. 2008; Hirschheim and Sabherwal 2001; Sabherwal et al. 2001).

In a longitudinal approach, the evolution of all aspects of the enterprise must be synchronized so that the alignment is continuous. However, it has been found that under-alignment or non-alignment are the most common situations (Hirschheim and Sabherwal 2001; Sabherwal et al. 2001). More specifically, it is difficult to maintain a high level of alignment for SMEs in a rapid growth phase (Chan et al. 2000).

The management of alignment over time is, in essence, a quest for coherence and synchronization. Sabherwal et al. (2001) make use of the theory of punctuated equilibrium in order to explain how the alignment is built. Their case studies show a combination of two dynamics: an incremental evolution toward greater alignment punctuated by radical changes that disrupt the context of alignment for the better or for the worst (Hirschheim and Sabherwal 2001).

The case study of a small semiconductor company in Taiwan conducted by Chen et al. (2000) sheds light on how an alignment is built over time. In the creation phase of the enterprise, strategies are vague and evolve quickly in order to seize opportunities; internal resources (i.e., skills and finance) are insufficient and IT is not a priority. In the growth phase, the company structures itself and investments in IT are more important. However, the alignment remains out of sync: the implementation of the desired alignment takes time, during which the strategy evolves. This is because when IT is not considered strategic, IT managers are not integrated into the strategic plan. Path dependency is also observed. Choices are dependent on previous investments which have not been optimized in the long term. The authors conclude that the theory of dynamic capabilities is a useful tool for studying the building of alignment over time. According to the authors, the ideal dynamic of alignment is based on the existence of a long-term IT strategy centered on IT resources, including a clear understanding of the business vision, and on the development of dynamic learning, integration and transformation, in order to reduce the lack of synchronization and the path dependency.

The major contribution of the longitudinal approach is to show that a situation of alignment is rare and difficult to maintain over time, and to study the mechanisms behind the building of alignment. To this end, the theories of dynamic capabilities (Chen et al. 2008) or punctuated equilibrium (Sabherwal et al. 2000) may be used. However, this approach is still not widely applied to the study of SMEs.

3.4.3. The co-evolution and the theory of complexity

For proponents of the theory of co-evolution, there is a rational and positivist illusion in the theories of alignment which focuses on simple causal relationships. This logic ignores the characteristics of a co-evolutionistic dynamic in the emergence of alignment. Several studies suggest that, in many cases, alignment is the result of a patchwork, even an accident, and is rationalized *a posteriori* (Benbya and McKelvey 2006; Peppard and Breu 2003). Co-evolution is based on the laws of complexity, and extends the systemic approach of alignment (Drazin and Van de Ven 1985).

Co-evolution is a multi-level dynamic. Macro co-evolution concerns the mutual influences between the organization and its environment. Micro co-evolution is experienced within the internal structure of a firm. (Peppard and Breu 2003). The latter involves the three levels, namely the individual, the operational and the strategic level (Benbya and McKelvey 2006). Causality is multi-directional and non-linear: an effect may have several causes, and these causes influence one another. Finally, changes are developed through positive feedback loops which create circular patterns of causality. According to the theory of co-evolution, the definition of IT alignment is the following:

> "IS alignment is a continuous co-evolutionary process that reconciles the rational top-down design and bottom-up emergent processes of consciously and coherently interrelating all components of the Business / IS relationship at three levels of analysis (strategic, operational and individual) in order to contribute to organizational performance over time." (Benbya and McKelve 2006, p. 287).

The theory of co-evolution as applied to the study of strategic alignment is still in its infancy. The contributions are theoretical at this stage. Peppard and Breu (2003) conclude that there is a need for an empirical verification of the model they have proposed. However, this theory is promising, as it extends the logic of systemic approaches of alignment by incorporating new variables (including individual and informal dimensions), deepening the dynamic relationships among variables, and by adopting a longitudinal approach.

The empirical literature supports the conclusion that, overall, there is a relationship between alignment and performance. However, when variables are introduced in order to create sub-samples (e.g., differences in strategies), this benefit is uneven with regard to the enterprise (Tallon 2008). In other words, the fact that an enterprise is aligned does not guarantee an impact on performance. In order to understand what explains the non-universality and non-uniformity of the impact of alignment on performance, it is necessary to break down the phenomenon of alignment, first vertically, by studying the necessary conditions for success (Burn and Szeto 2000; Chan et al. 2006; Reich and Benbasat 2000) and then going down to the level of the micro-alignment of processes (Tallon 2008), then horizontally through a longitudinal approach (Hirschheim and Sabherwal 2001; Sabherwal et al. 2001) or through a co-evolutionist approach (Benbya and McKelvay 2006; Chen et al. 2008; Peppard and Breu 2003).

4. Factors involved in the building of alignment

In order to better understand this phenomenon, a stream of literature focuses on the antecedent factors which have an impact on the building of alignment. The factors identified are grouped under three dimensions. The social dimension involves four factors: confidence in the IT function, the competence of the IT function, the competence and knowledge of the IT function in conjunction with other functions of the organization, and finally the management culture. The project dimension involves three factors: the existence of a clear vision and strategic orientations, IT leadership from the decision-maker, and proximity between the leaders and the IT function. Finally, the process of IT management has an important impact on the building of alignment through three factors: the formalization of the IT planning process, the change management of the IT function of and the innovation strategy in the use of IT.

These factors have been identified in a part of the literature that is almost exclusively focused on large enterprises. Some of these factors are not adapted to the context of SMEs. For example, the majority of SMEs have no internal IT specialist. Additionally, in many SMEs, strategy is not formalized. Strategy is often "in the head" of the leader and it is usually more emergent than planned. This underlines the need to develop analytical frameworks specific to SMEs.

In the following subsections, we identify the key points of each factor.

4.1. Confidence, competence, IT culture

The social dimension has received less attention from researchers (Reich and Benbasat 2000). Two factors are key: the perception that the organization has of the IT function and the existence of a joint knowledge between the IT function and the rest of the organization. They determine both the role that is attributed to the IT function and its role in the business discussions: is it perceived as a player capable of having a strategic contribution, capable of influencing the definition of the strategy, or is it seen as an implementation service with little organizational influence?

This image is being built, in particular, on the history of achievements in IT implementation (Chan et al. 2006; Reich and Benbasat 2000). The existence of a joint knowledge between IT and business also plays a significant role (Chan et al. 2006), both in the building of an alignment in the short term and in the long term (Reich and Benbasat 2000). Reich and Benbasat (2000) even find that in the long run, only the common sharing of knowledge can distinguish the top performing enterprises from the others. Mutual influence is possible among IT and non-IT managers when IT managers understand the issues, opportunities and threats of the industry sector and of the organization, and when the non-IT managers have a sufficient knowledge of IT. Mutual influence is required to develop a common vision and to set priorities.

A history of failure may be offset in a context where there exists a shared vision between the IT function and the organization, and when the joint knowledge is rich (Reich and Benbasat 2000). The competencies of the IT function are also a factor affecting its credibility and influence. Reich and Benbasat (2000) stress, in particular, the ability to communicate with the rest of the organization, which is a complex task for a highly technical profession in constant evolution.

4.2. The existence of a strategic project

The existence of a long term vision and clear short term direction also facilitates the development of alignment (Chan and Reich 2007; Reich and Benbasat 2000). The role of the leader is another important factor. The leader's support is clearly needed in the alignment process. The leader's relationship with the person in charge of IT plays an important role in the building of joint knowledge and a relationship of trust and mutual influence (Chan and Reich 2007). In one organizations studied by Reich and Benbasat (2000), the influence of a leader who was very competent in IT and who possessed strong leadership skills was crucial to the building of alignment in the organization as a whole.

4.3. A rigorous planning process

For many authors, the existence of an IT planning process is a must in order to achieve alignment (Chan and Reich 2007). An IT planning process has five phases: the framing of the process, the situation analysis, the strategic design, the strategy formulation and the planning of the implementation (Newkirk et al. 2008). By structuring the planning process, the organization makes sure that the exchange of information and the mutual influence will be higher, while, at the same time, it defines the role of each actor (Burn and Szeto 2000; Chan et al. 2006; Chan and Reich 2007).

Other studies lead to more nuanced conclusions. The existence of a formal planning process generally favors the development of alignment (Burn and Szeto 2000; Croteau and Bergeron 2001; Newkirk et al. 2008). However, this is not a direct effect (Chan et al. 2006). All phases of such a process do not directly affect the alignment (Newkirk et al. 2008). A formal process has an impact on the alignment in the short term in that it allows the enterprise to decide on priorities and plan the implementation. However, its effect on alignment in the long term is fuzzy since alignment also results from a long built social interaction between IT players and the rest of the organization (Reich and Benbasat 2000).

3.4. Alignment factors differentiated in terms of strategies

The factors that have an impact on the building of the alignment are obviously not identical in all enterprises. Firm size has an impact on the alignment process. In SMEs, proximity facilitates the informal exchange of information and centralized decision-making. On the contrary, coordination is more complex in a large company and the establishment of a formal alignment process is required (Chan et al. 2006).

The adopted strategy also has an effect. Thus, an enterprise that adopts a strategy of defense in the typology of Miles and Snow is sensitive to the uncertainty of the environment and to the history of IT success, while prospectors and analysts who are more adventurous and outward-oriented are less sensitive to these conditions (Chan et al. 2006).

5. Research directions

The literature on IT strategic alignment has many gray areas. The models used integrate only some of the factors explaining the link between IT strategic alignment and performance. It is therefore necessary to adopt a systemic approach and to integrate new variables which influence the relationship between alignment and performance. We propose seven areas of research: SMEs specificities, emerging strategies, external alignment, building alignments, social network and knowledge management, change management, and alignment on business model.

5.1. SMEs specificities

With regard to strategic management, SMEs have several specificities. The first is related to the limited financial and human resources. Unlike large companies, very often, SMEs do not have an IT service, but merely some technical support positions. Another major difference in a small business is that the owner-manager has a key role in developing the strategy. Most often, owner-managers embody the vision of their companies. This vision often mirrors their own life ambitions. The business strategy is rarely formalized. This is because SMEs often have reactive strategies that adapt in order to seize opportunities and counter threats, especially in the early stages of development (Chen et al. 2008). Another reason is that the vision is in the mind of the owner. The leader also has a critical role with respect to key operational decisions in alignment: the decisions concerning IT, resource allocation, management of organizational structure, etc. Thus, the owner plays a major role in the building of alignment.

Yet, to the best of our knowledge, a strategic alignment model developed specifically for SMEs does not exist. The SAM (Strategic

Alignment Model) of Henderson and Venkatraman (1993), the most widely used in the literature, is based on the examples of large enterprises, and does not take into account the particularities of SMEs. Hence, a first area of research would concern the development of a conceptual framework for IT alignment that is designed specifically for SMEs.

5.2. Emerging strategy

Methods of strategy development are also evolving. In the current environment of socio-economic chaos, planning is a perilous exercise. Strategy development is increasingly becoming a constant work in progress which is being built in a double dynamic. The strategy is imposed from above, particularly through operational decisions (e.g., resource allocation, process implementation), and it emerges from the decisions made by operational managers due to their changing environment. In this context, the desired strategy and the implemented strategy are rarely synchronous, but in a state of permanent mutual influence. In this context, the IT alignment on the desired strategy, i.e. the formal strategy, may paradoxically appear as an obstacle to the success of an emerging strategy. Indeed, it requires a technological infrastructure that is not necessarily tailored to the needs of adapting to a chaotic environment.

At the extreme, it is even possible to ask whether IT strategic alignment is desirable for an SME. Indeed, the competitive advantage for a SME is based on its strategic agility, i.e., its ability to react quickly in order to seize opportunities. Rather than trying to align the IT functions to the desired strategy, would it not be preferable for an SME to develop a "tight coupling" of capabilities in order to adjust the IT infrastructure to a continuously emerging strategy. In other words, is a tight coupling of emerging strategies with IT capabilities better than a coupling of IT capabilities with the desired strategy? The evolution of technologies, including web-based technologies, offers new possibilities in this direction.

5.3. External alignment

Alignment models focus primarily on analyzing internal alignment. For example, Henderson and Venkatraman (1993) consider partnerships and alliances as a means of access to IT skills. Today, the network is at the heart of strategies for value creation in SMEs. Supply chain partners are increasingly intertwined due to information exchange, collaborative design, order management and inventory. The position of a SME in the supply chain of its sector, as well as the nature of its relationship with its suppliers, partners and customers, has a decisive impact on its needs for technology infrastructure. In particular, the needs of its largest customers may force a SME to implement certain IT functions (Croteau et al. 2007).

From this point of view, the alignment should not only be analyzed from an internal point of view, but it must integrate the dimensions of alignment with the network of partners. In this context, the governance mechanisms of the IT network, in terms of structure, formal mechanisms, participants and informal mechanisms, are important factors to be considered.

5.4. Building alignments

The literature supports the conclusion that the overall alignment between business strategies and IT has an impact on performance. Yet when we look at this in detail, either, by micro-level processes or by adopting multivariate methods, the reality is more nuanced, if not paradoxical, and the reasons for this are unclear (Chan et al. 2006). Understanding how alignment is built in SMEs in order to, in turn, understand how to create performance, is therefore a very relevant line of research.

Three approaches can be exploited. Systemic approaches expand the scope of investigation by incorporating additional variables such as social dynamics, informal realities, and network strategy. Their inclusion in the study of the alignment could contribute to increase the alignment explanatory potential. The study of alignment at a micro level asks for a breakdown of the structure of alignment. It allows the study of the basic elements of alignment, such as processes (Tallon 2008). Finally, the longitudinal approach allows us to understand the evolution of alignment over time.

5.5. Social networks and knowledge management

Aside from the question of competencies, social dimensions are under-represented in the analysis alignment models. However, two antecedents of alignment are frequently cited: joint knowledge and the confidence gained from past implementation. Social networks, the relationships with the consultants, are key factors in the building of alignment (Chan and

Reich 2007). Several researchers have introduced the concept of knowledge management in the alignment process (Benbya and McKelvey 2006; Hirschheim and Sabherwal 2001).

The literature on knowledge management has largely studied the phenomena of information exchange and knowledge in a process of IT implementation (Jones 2005; Ko et al. 2005; Li et al. 2006; Maguire et al. 2007; McGinnis and Huang 2007; Palanisamy 2007; Pan et al. 2006). Because SMEs have limited internal competencies, they are dependent on their ability to internalize knowledge in order to build the alignment of their IT. Therefore, the integration of formal and informal mechanisms for information sharing appears to be an interesting approach that can be used to refine the understanding of alignment.

5.6. Change management

A major cause of frequent ICT implementation failure is that change management is not adequately planned, and that the real reasons for resistance to the introduction of new systems are not taken into account (Newkirk et al. 2008). Even if the best IT decisions are made, it doesn't necessarily follow that the employees will adopt the technology. Many cognitive and psychological factors must be taken into account (Venkatesh et al. 2003).

Managing the human aspect of change is, therefore, a key condition for success (Benbya and McKelvey 2006; Chan and Reich 2007). The study of the link between change management and IT alignment is, thus, a dimension that should be looked at more closely in order to understand how to create performance.

5.7. Alignment on business model

Six elements define a business model: the organization of the offer (products, services), the target market segments, the supply chain structure, the financial mechanism of income generation, the network configuration, the strategy adopted (Chesbrough 2007). The business model is a holistic concept that describes all the variables that constitute what the organization is, and how it does business.

A better understanding of the alignment issue requires adopting a systemic approach (Drazin and Van de Ven 1985). In order to generate performance, IT must be aligned with all the variables constituting the business model of the organization. Thus, we are less concerned with the study of IT strategic alignment than we are with the alignment of IT with the business model. We suggest a change of perspective that is consistent with the need for a systemic approach; we propose to emphasize the IT alignment on the business model rather than focusing on the IT alignment on the sole business strategy.

Conclusion

A review of the literature on the relationship between IT strategic alignment and performance highlights some conclusions, while at the same time revealing a number of gray areas. The first conclusion is that the alignment between business strategies and IT has an overall positive impact on performance. However, when we go further into detail and take into account the business strategies pursued or the effects of the entire system, it appears that this positive effect is neither universal nor uniform. In order to better understand the alignment, several approaches have emerged. The systemic approach incorporates more variables and takes into account the relationships between these variables. The longitudinal approach introduces the temporal dimension and shows that the alignment implies the synchronization of strategy and its management. We propose seven areas of research: SMEs specificities, emerging strategies, external alignment, building alignments, social network and knowledge management, change management, and alignment on business model. Practitioners stand to gain the benefit of increased performance and to achieve a sustainable competitive advantage from these research areas.

CHAPTER FOUR

QUALITATIVE PREDICTING E-SALES EVOLUTION: IDENTIFYING E-COMMERCE SUCCESS FACTORS AND MODELING THEIR IMPACT USING A RULE-BASED DSS

LUCA CANETTA, NAOUFEL CHEIKHROUHOU AND RÉMY GLARDON

Introduction

The share of e-commerce in business is still increasing at a fast pace, considering both business-to-business (B2B) or business-to-consumer (B2C) transactions. However, e-commerce is not yet mature and thus is far from reaching its steady state potential. The uncertainties related to e-commerce adoption are confirmed by the large differences in the predictions provided by various organizations in charge of monitoring its future evolution (Gurunlian and Zhoungzhou 2001). An increasing number of companies are confronted with the decision of whether to adopt electronically enabled sales channels (e-sales channels) to replace and/or support their traditional channels. They are motivated by the fact that the adoption of a multi-channel sales strategy seems promising both in terms of sales and revenue increase (Roland et al. 2000). Nevertheless, the decisions and changes required by e-commerce introduction are complex and can have a critical impact on the achievement of sustainable competitive advantage. The high degree of uncertainty concerning customer reactions to e-commerce further complicates the choice of an adequate e-sales strategy and also contributes to the uneven utilization of online purchasing across different industrial sectors (Stansfield and Grant 2003; Selhofer 2004). The high risks characterizing the introduction of an e-commerce strategy can be explained by the potential critical impact of the e-strategy on company revenue and operating cost, and therefore on its overall wealth. Many companies are therefore hesitant about implementing an e-strategy in order to take full advantage of the benefits of the e-revolution. This demonstrates the necessity to reduce the complexity of the decisions concerning e-strategy identification and implementation, as well as to develop tools that support the company management during these processes.

This chapter aims to identify the attributes influencing customer willingness to adopt e-purchasing and to formalize the relationships between these attributes. Furthermore, another objective is to provide a description of e-purchasing adoption characteristics, based on the application of Diffusion of Innovation (DOI) models. Determining customer e-purchasing behavior is essential for companies considering new e-sales channel introduction, as it allows them to estimate the e-sales amount that can be potentially reached by targeting these customers.

The next section provides a description of the overall approach and then in section 2, the list of the identified e-commerce success factors is presented. The preliminary results of a Delphi study, that allows estimating the impact of each e-commerce success factor, are analyzed in section 3. The various rule sets involving linguistic variables, presented in detail in section 4, allow companies to qualitatively predict the potential e-sales evolution of a given company applying a specific e-commerce strategy. Finally, in section 5, the findings of this work are summarized and some research perspectives are outlined.

1. Proposed approach

This work is primarily focused on B2B e-commerce. This is motivated by the fact that it already accounts for about 80% of the monetary value of total e-commerce transactions and that it is expected to have a faster growth than B2C (Scupola 2002).

The proposed approach is articulated into three phases (Figure 4-1). First, the factors that have a significant impact on e-purchasing adoption are identified through a detailed analysis of the e-commerce literature. The main factors, called e-commerce success factors in the remainder of this work include: the nature of the transacted products or services, the characteristics of the targeted customers, of the available e-sales channels and of the selling company.

Second, the magnitude and the direction of the influence of each e-commerce success factor, already partially provided by the literature analysis (Canetta et al. 2007), is further analyzed and validated based on the opinions of an expert panel. A Delphi study was designed and developed to collect expert opinions. This technique was chosen because it has already proven to be suitable for the evaluation of e-commerce related subjects (Addison 2003; Holzmüller and Schluchter 2002; Huang et al. 2005; Lee and Li 2006; Okoli and Pawlowski 2004). Furthermore, the recourse to a Delphi study addresses potential incongruences/ambiguities that sometimes characterize the descriptions of the impact of e-commerce success factors provided in the analyzed literature; this is due to the use of different definitions and/or to the lack of sufficient data about e-commerce (Ewton 2003).

Finally, in order to provide an effective modeling of the evolution of the company's e-sales using the findings of the previous steps, the various rule sets constituting the DSS are formalized. The identified e-commerce success factors are the inputs of the rule-based DSS. The DSS outputs, the parameters to be used for qualitative modeling the e-sales evolution, are defined based on a literature review. In particular, works dealing with the application of DOI mathematical models to Information and Communication Technology (ICT) and e-commerce adoption description (Rai et al. 1998; Samaddar et al. 2002; Teng et al. 2002) are investigated in order to provide the required DSS outputs. The rule sets are then formalized using the preliminary results of a Delphi study and the rules established by the authors in a previous work (Canetta et al. 2007).

The proposed DSS explains how a specific market configuration, described in terms of e-commerce success factor values, leads to a given e-sales evolution. It is qualitatively modeled using DOI theory (Rogers 1995) in terms of saturation level (share of e-purchasing at the end of the innovation diffusion process) and speed of adoption (number of periods necessary to reach the saturation level). Product features, customer characteristics, brand perception and e-commerce induced process modifications are simultaneously taken into account for describing the e-sales evolution.

In order to facilitate the parameterization of the DSS, in particular for users belonging to companies not already familiar with e-commerce, and considering that in the current version it provides just a qualitative description, each configuration of e-commerce success factors is described using linguistic variables. This choice is coherent with the approach used in judgment and qualitative information assessment, as well as for the analysis of immature technologies, for which quantitative data are difficult to obtain and which do not yet provide a reliable prediction of their future evolution (Bradley and Stewart 2003; Okoli and Pawlowski 2004).

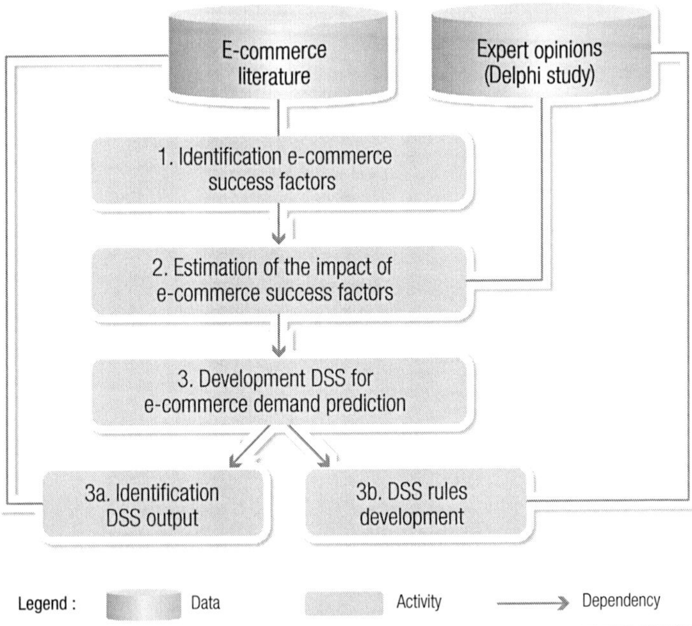

Figure 4-1 Approach for the development of a rule-based DSS for e-sales evolution qualitative prediction

2. Identification of e-commerce success factors

The important differences characterizing e-commerce adoption both at the single company and at the industrial sector level have been extensively investigated. Several interpretations have been proposed to explain these discrepancies and to identify which characteristics ensure a rapid and massive e-purchasing adoption. The explanation of the e-commerce adoption process is mainly based on the analysis of customer perception (Choi et al. 2004; Levin et al. 2003; Liang and Huang 1998; Lim 2003;

Liu and Wei 2003; Schaupp and Bélanger 2005; Vijayasarathy 2002; Zhou et al. 2004). Previous research has applied Transaction Cost Analysis (TCA) (Kiang et al. 2000; Liang and Huang 1998; Santarelli and D'Altri 2001), risk perception and trust analysis (Hassanein and Head 2004; Lim 2003; Srinivasan 2004), Diffusion of Innovation theory (DOI) (Kendall et al. 2001; Skjevdal et al. 2004; Wright et al. 1997), and Technology Acceptance Model (TAM) (Liu and Wei 2003; Wetzels 2003). Many of these exploratory analyses are qualitative in nature and focus only on a subset of the factors that potentially influence e-purchasing adoption. Many works have emphasized the importance of the e-commerce suitability of the transacted products (Hunter et al. 2004; Levin et al., 2003; Liu and Wei, 2003; Liu et al., 2004; Lowengart and Tractinsky 2001; Peterson et al. 1997; Phau and Poon 2000; Vijayasarathy 2002). Another recurrent aspect is the focus on ICT infrastructure availability and, more generally, customer readiness to adopt e-commerce (Choi et al. 2004; Fillis et al. 2003; Liang and Huang 1998; Scupola 2002; Selhofer 2004; Zhou et al. 2004). The role of brand image, due to its ability to at least partially leverage customer risk perception, has also retained the attention of various researchers (Bendixen et al. 2004; Clemons and Aron 2002; Lim 2003; Mudambi 2002). In this section a further step is undertaken in order to identify most of the e-commerce success factors, more precisely the attributes that have a significant impact on e-purchasing adoption. These attributes are related to product and to customer characteristics as well as to the purchasing process modifications related to the proposed e-sales channels. Furthermore, the importance of brand perception, in particular for new potential customers (not belonging to the current customer base), is taken into account. The identification of the e-commerce success factors is based on a literature review, which comprises contributions from both B2B and B2C research fields, thus allowing access to a wide article selection.

2.1 Product features

Evidences of the moderating effect of product and service characteristics on e-commerce adoption willingness can be found in the literature (Levin et al. 2003; Liu and Wei 2003; Liu et al. 2004 Lowengart and Tractinsky 2001; Peterson et al. 1997; Phau and Poon 2000; Vijayasarathy 2002). Product features can influence perceived risk (Hassanein and Head 2004; Lim 2003; Liu and Wei 2003), transaction costs (Liu and Wei 2003; Lowengart and Tractinsky 2001; Santarelli and D'Altri 2001) and level of trust (Hassanein and Head 2004). The analyzed literature clearly shows the importance of the following four product characteristics, which are among the most cited: degree of intangibility, importance, degree of membership to the search goods class and degree of standardization.

2.1.1 Degree of intangibility

Intangibility has proven to influence e-commerce adoption both in B2B (Liu et al. 2004) and B2C market environments (Liu and Wei 2003; Peterson et al. 1997; Phau and Poon 2000; Vijayasarathy 2002). Intangibility measures the lack of physical evidence, for this reason it has been originally used for distinguishing goods from services. Intangibility describes the difficulty to assess or test a given product/service prior to purchasing. On the one hand, intangibility can be a barrier to e-commerce when dealing with physical products because, in contrast to retail outlets, the product cannot be touched (Featherman and Wells 2004). On the other hand, e-sales channels seem well suited for transacting intangible products due to transaction cost reductions made possible by their instantaneous electronic delivery (Liu and Wei 2003). Moreover, instantaneous electronic delivery decreases the uncertainty concerning the quality of goods, which can be assessed more rapidly than using traditional sales channels (Liu and Wei 2003). In this context, intangibility refers specifically to the nature of products; it is thus expected to have a positive effect due to its contribution to reducing the perceived risk.

2.1.2. Importance

Product importance can be defined as the "degree of essentiality" of the supplier delivery to the organization, as perceived by the buyer (Hunter et al. 2004). High product importance increases perceived risk, thus it has a negative effect on e-purchasing adoption. Perceived risk is recognized as an important hindering factor for online shopping (Lim 2003; Liu et al. 2004). Product importance influences the magnitude of the undesirable consequences, mainly due to financial and performance risk, and the likelihood of negative outcomes. The costs and losses resulting from quality problems, delay problems and other uncertainties are thought to be directly dependent on product importance. The B2C literature indicates high product price as a factor hindering e-commerce adoption (Lim 2003; Lowengart and Tractinsky 2001; Peterson et al. 1997; Phau and Poon 2000; Vijayasarathy 2002). However, in a B2B marketplace both financial and performance risks are significant; this therefore requires a comprehensive evaluation of product importance. In the B2B literature, this is usually assessed by the dichotomies between low importance products, such as commodities and MRO (Maintenance, Repair and Operations), and important products, such as direct customized materials. The hypothesis that a higher product importance hinders e-commerce adoption is confirmed by the wider diffusion of e-purchasing for MRO products than for direct materials (Hunter et al. 2004).

2.1.3. Degree of membership to the search goods class

Search goods can be completely assessed without a physical inspection, because their features and characteristics are easily observable before purchase. On the other hand, one or more characteristics of an experience good, such as quality or price, are difficult to observe in advance and can only be ascertained upon consumption or, at least, physical inspection. Search goods can be more easily described through a website than experience ones, because all relevant data and characteristics can be provided before transaction fulfillment. In this way, the customer's perceived risk is drastically reduced for search goods e-purchasing (Clemons and Aron 2002). The degree of membership in the search goods class is expected to have a pronounced positive impact on e-purchasing adoption, as already stated by previous works (Choi et al. 2004; Clemons and Aron 2002; Levin et al. 2003; Peterson et al. 1997; Phau and Poon 2000). For instance, Levin (Levin et al. 2003) investigates how the degree of membership in the search goods class changes the importance of various shopping attributes as well as customer preferences between online and offline sales channels.

2.1.4. Degree of standardization

In a B2B environment, a high degree of standardization reduces the need for physical inspection of the product (Clemons and Aron 2002; Liang and Huang 1998) and the amount of information necessary for making a purchasing decision (Hunter et al. 2004; Tsao and Lin 2001). This results in a reduction of the customer's perceived risk that facilitates e-purchasing adoption for highly standardized products. Thus, in this work, the degree of standardization is expected to have a positive effect on e-purchasing adoption.

2.2. Customer characteristics

The great attention dedicated by several organizations to the gathering and analysis of customer related indicators, with the aim of assessing customer e-commerce readiness (Gurunlian and Zhongzhou 2001; Selhofer 2004), points to the importance of the relationships between customer characteristics and e-commerce adoption. Evidence of this relationship can be found in (Liu et al. 2004; Scupola 2002; Selhofer 2004; Stansfield and Grant 2003). Four characteristics appear to play an important role in explaining the behaviour of customers involved in B2B e-commerce: ICT resources, e-commerce experience, e-sales channel evaluation and purchasing frequency.

2.2.1. ICT resources

Lack of ICT resources can become an entry barrier for companies interested in e-commerce, especially for small and medium sized enterprises (SMEs), (Fillis et al. 2003; Stansfield and Grant 2003). The magnitude of the differences among e-commerce adopters and non adopters also depends on the sophistication of the considered ICT. While basic ICT (computers, internet and e-mail) are widely adopted even by companies not involved in e-commerce (Selhofer 2004), significant differences exist between e-commerce adopters and non-adopters when considering data about IT staff, ICT training and ICT knowledge (Fillis et al. 2003; Scupola 2002). It seems that SMEs and more generally non-adopters and weak adopters lack the knowledge about the Internet and electronic commerce which is necessary to make the leap towards full integration (Stansfield and Grant 2003). In other words, the strongest barrier to e-commerce take-up by SMEs is constituted by the lack of skilled IT staff.

The data, from a survey performed in 2003 by the e-Business W@tch (Selhofer 2004), describes the characteristics of a sample of 4,326 European companies involved in B2B transactions, have been analyzed to confirm the theoretical findings. The percentage of utilization of various ICT resources and IT activities are estimated for four classes of companies, obtained by splitting the sample according to the current share of e-purchasing (calculated as a percentage of the overall purchases). In this way, the four classes are defined as intensive e-purchasing adopters (share >26%), average adopters (5-25%), weak adopters (<5%) and non-adopters.

The results of this analysis, provided in Table 4-1, point out the following tendencies:

- Some basic ICT tools (e-mail and World Wide Web) are used at a lower level by non-adopters (almost 55% of the sample);
- Almost all e-purchasing companies master basic ICT tools whatever their share of e-purchasing;
- Compared to average and intensive e-purchasing adopters, companies belonging to the weak adopter class (22% of the sample) lag behind in terms of adoption of the more advanced ICT tools (Intranet, Extranet, LAN, Wireless LAN), as well as in terms of a thorough knowledge regarding more challenging activities (IT training, IT staff recruiting, company website).

The results, as well as the analyzed literature, show that available ICT resources have a positive influence on e-purchasing adoption. However, the predicted smoothing of the differences in ICT resources and knowledge among companies in many industrial sectors tends to render its future impact on e-commerce diffusion less prominent.

Share of e-purchasing		>26%	5-25%	< 5%	No
Basic ICT	Use computer	100.00	100.00	100.00	100.00
	Internet access	100.00	99.70	99.47	92.65
	E-mail	100.00	98.51	99.05	88.51
	WWW	98.52	95.96	94.01	79.22
Advanced ICT	Intranet	63.31	60.84	50.37	34.38
	Extranet	32.25	20.70	18.19	12.42
	LAN	86.39	80.87	73.61	51.60
	Wireless LAN	36.09	35.43	24.08	15.96
IT training & learning	In-house IT training	54.70	55.16	50.79	35.14
	Third party IT	62.43	61.14	55.42	39.23
	Personal learning	81.77	79.37	67.61	48.44
IT staff recruiting		41.44	32.44	21.66	11.91
Corporate Website		82.32	83.11	75.50	57.56

Table 4-1 B2B customer characteristics [all data in %]

2.2.2. E-commerce (e-purchasing) experience

Customer perceived risk and thus customer willingness to adopt e-purchasing are also influenced by the positive impact of previous successful e-commerce experiences through the "learning effect in electronic commerce" (Liang and Huang 1998). This attribute captures all the past e-commerce experiences of the customer and takes into account the confidence and skills developed across them. Vijayasarathy states that successful e-commerce experience has a strong positive influence on future shopping intentions (Vijayasarathy 2002). Naturally, this positive effect exists for e-suppliers for which transactions have already taken place. However, it also spreads its beneficial influence, at least partially, to new unknown suppliers as well as to the purchasing of products not already bought on line. Experienced customers are thus more willing to adopt e-purchasing than inexperienced ones.

2.2.3. E-sales channels evaluation

The attribute e-sales channel evaluation focuses on a dyadic customer-supplier relationship and points out a more specific aspect of customer attitude towards e-purchasing than the previously described e-commerce experience. This attribute, which takes into account the perceived usefulness (relative advantage) and ease of use (simplicity and compatibility) of the available e-sales channels, appears to significantly influence the willingness to adopt e-commerce (Choi et al. 2004). The overall evaluation of the perceived quality of a specific e-sales channel, both in comparison with traditional sales channels, (Levin et al. 2003) as well as with other types of e-sales channels (Choi et al. 2004; Lowengart and Tractinsky 2001), takes into account a great number of features. Furthermore, many of these features often show strong correlations and tradeoffs between them which requires the use of sophisticated techniques in order to provide reliable estimations.

Conjoint Analysis has been proposed by Schaupp and Bélanger (2005) to evaluate online customer satisfaction in a B2C environment. Similarly, Canetta et al. (2004) proposes and tests a Conjoint Analysis based approach to estimate the importance of purchasing process modifications, available e-services and customer adoption efforts in a B2B environment. The obtained results demonstrate how the preference structure of customers can differ significantly, resulting in the choice of different e-sales channels, as well as how the estimation of customer preferences constitutes an important input for evaluating the profitability of a given e-commerce strategy before implementing it.

The good fit between the features of the available channel and customer needs implies a positive e-sales channel evaluation. Thus this attribute is expected to have a strong positive influence on customer willingness to adopt e-purchasing.

2.2.4. Purchasing frequency

The decision to adopt a particular e-sales channel stems from the comparison of its perceived usefulness (for instance transaction cost reduction) with the customer's efforts required to implement it (ranging from the ICT investments to the loss of productivity due to the learning effect). E-purchasing adoption decision is thus highly influenced by customer purchasing frequency. In fact, only a sufficiently high purchasing frequency can leverage the required investments by reaching a critical mass that ensures the profitability of e-purchasing adoption. The relevance of purchasing frequency on e-purchasing adoption is empirically demonstrated by previous studies in both B2C (Peterson et al. 1997; Phau and Poon 2000) and B2B e-commerce (Subramaniam and Shaw 2002).

2.3. Purchasing process modifications

Customer perceived usefulness is considered as one of the main drivers of innovation adoption by both TAM (Davis 1989) and DOI (Rogers 1995) theories. E-purchasing perceived usefulness is mainly related to the significant customer buying process modifications induced by the adoption of a particular e-sales channel configuration. While assessing the impact of process modifications, it is important to ensure a sufficient broad vision, including production, distribution, inventory management and order-handling processes (Clemons and Aron 2002; Iliev et al. 2004; Jansen et al. 2004; Subramaniam and Shaw 2002).

2.4. Brand perception

Brand perception influences customer satisfaction and intention to purchase both in the B2B (Bendixen et al. 2004) and in B2C (Levin et al. 2003) marketplaces. Especially for new potential customers, who are characterized by experiencing high levels of risk and uncertainty, brand perception leverages the perceived risk of e-commerce transactions. The positive effect of brand perception for customers belonging to the current customer base is mitigated by the fact that the latter have already acquired knowledge about product characteristics and supplier performance during their previous transactions and thus are characterised by a smaller level of perceived risk. As previously stated, brand perception is expected to play a significant role for new potential customers. For this reason this attribute is only used to describe the e-purchasing adoption process for this class of customers. Three factors have been identified as suitable for describing brand perception: brand awareness, brand perception and "distance".

2.4.1. Brand awareness

Brand awareness, the degree to which target customers recall a brand or are aware of its existence, provides a measure of marketing communication effectiveness. Brand awareness facilitates e-purchasing adoption, reducing perceived risk and uncertainty, especially for customers belonging to market segments not already covered by the current customer base. It constitutes a significant risk reliever, as stated by Van den Poel and Leunis (1999) who ranks well-known brands as the second most important characteristic just behind a money-back guarantee.

2.4.2. Brand reputation

Brand reputation has a great positive influence on customer willingness to adopt e-purchasing (Clemons and Aron 2002; Lim 2003), because it measures the perceived quality associated with the brand by customers. Even more than brand awareness, brand reputation, also called brand image, can improve customer trust and leverage perceived risk and uncertainty.

2.4.3. Distance

Distance is introduced to take into account that the perception of brand related attributes varies across customers and purchasing situations (Mudambi 2002). Distance not only takes buyer and seller respective geographical locations into account, but also other differences between characteristics of the new potential customer in comparison to those of the current customer base. For instance, a new potential buyer belonging to an industrial sector, radically different from those usually targeted by the seller, suffers from a lack of knowledge that increases perceived risk. Distance captures the difficulty for a new potential buyer to already know the seller and assess its performances; it is thus expected to have a negative impact on brand perception and to hinder e-purchasing adoption.

3. Estimation of the impact of the e-commerce success factors

The magnitude and the direction of the influence of the previously identified e-commerce success factors are assessed/validated using the opinions of an expert panel. In this section, a brief description of the characteristics of the Delphi study used and of its specific application to e-commerce analysis is provided, before presenting the obtained results.

3.1. Delphi study

Delphi studies are usually employed when judgmental information is indispensable, especially in the context of complex decision and analysis of industries undergoing rapid changes (Bradley and Stewart 2003; Okoli and Pawlowsky 2004). The Delphi method aims at structuring a group communication process and allowing a systematic pooling of the expert panel opinions through iterative questionnaires, referred to as “rounds”. At the end of each round, a summarized feedback of the previous round’s responses is sent to panelists who are asked to reconsider their own answers on the basis of this supplementary information. Furthermore, asking respondents to justify their responses, especially for those sustaining opinions diverging from those of the majority of the experts, can improve the understanding of the causal relationships between factors and/or emphasize differences of opinion in order to develop a set of alternative future scenarios to be further analyzed.

Evidences of the superiority of Delphi method, compared to other group judgment techniques, are given in various works (Catell 2002; Okoli and Pawlowsky 2004) and are mainly related to the anonymity of the experts and by the avoidance of direct confrontation among them, which reduces the bias usually involved in face-to face contact (Addison 2003; Cabaniss 2001).

In this work a variant of the original Delphi method, called modified (Cabaniss 2001) or ranking type (Okoli and Pawlowsky 2004) Delphi, is applied. It specifically consists in replacing the open-ended questions in the first round by a list of attributes to be rated. The selection of the expert panel, size and composition, is one of the most important steps. According to previous recommendations, the panel should contain at least seven respondents (Bradley and Stewart, 2003), with a typical size of 10-20 experts (Cabaniss 2001; Okoli and Pawlowsky 2004). In the present work the selected panel is composed of 18 experts, selected among academics and practitioners, mostly from Western Europe and North America.

The results of the first round of the Delphi study are presented in this work; they give meaningful indications due to the high degree of convergence already achieved for many e-commerce success factors. The direction and the magnitude of the impact of e-commerce success factors have been estimated on the basis of the Delphi results using the following notation: (2) very positive, (1) positive, (0) not significant, (-1) negative, (-2) very negative, (DK) do not know.

In order to extract as much information as possible from the expert answers various indexes describing the overall panel opinions, are provided. First, the following statistical measures were calculated: average, median and mode. Then, a graph, showing the percentage of experts choosing each of the 5 impact levels as well as those preferring not to answer due to lack of knowledge, provides an even more detailed description of the expert opinions and of their degree of convergence. All this information is taken into account in establishing the impact of the e-commerce success factors.

3.2. Product features

The findings about the impact of the different features of a product for its e-commerce suitability are contrasted. A sufficient degree of convergence has been obtained for degree of membership to the search goods class and for standardization level, as shown in Figure 4-2. Furthermore, the expert opinions comply well with the theoretical evidence, assigning a very positive impact to standardization and a positive impact to the membership of the search goods class. On the other hand, opinions on the impact of intangibility and importance still diverge, due to apparently counterintuitive answers given by a few experts. This can be explained by the different impact that these factors can have on perceived risk, for instance depending on the specific market environment to be analyzed. Due to the lack of experts' agreement, the impacts of intangibility and of importance will be estimated on the basis of the literature review (section 2.1) respectively as positive and negative.

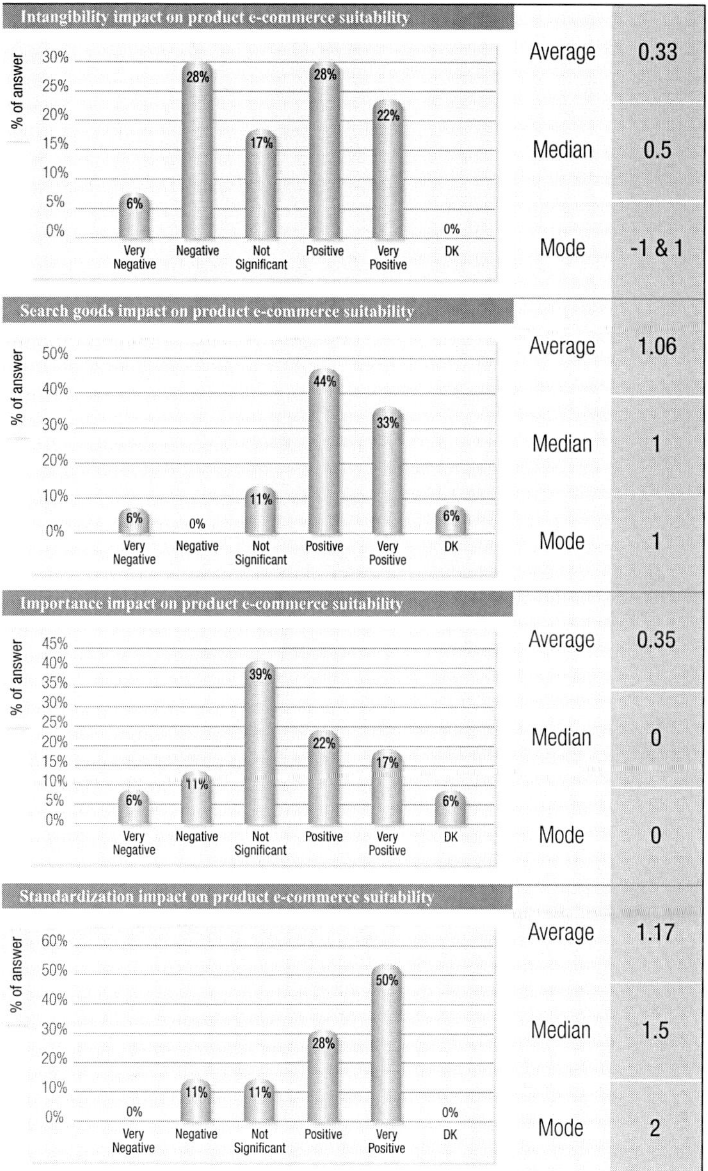

Figure 4-2 Product features impact on product e-commerce suitability

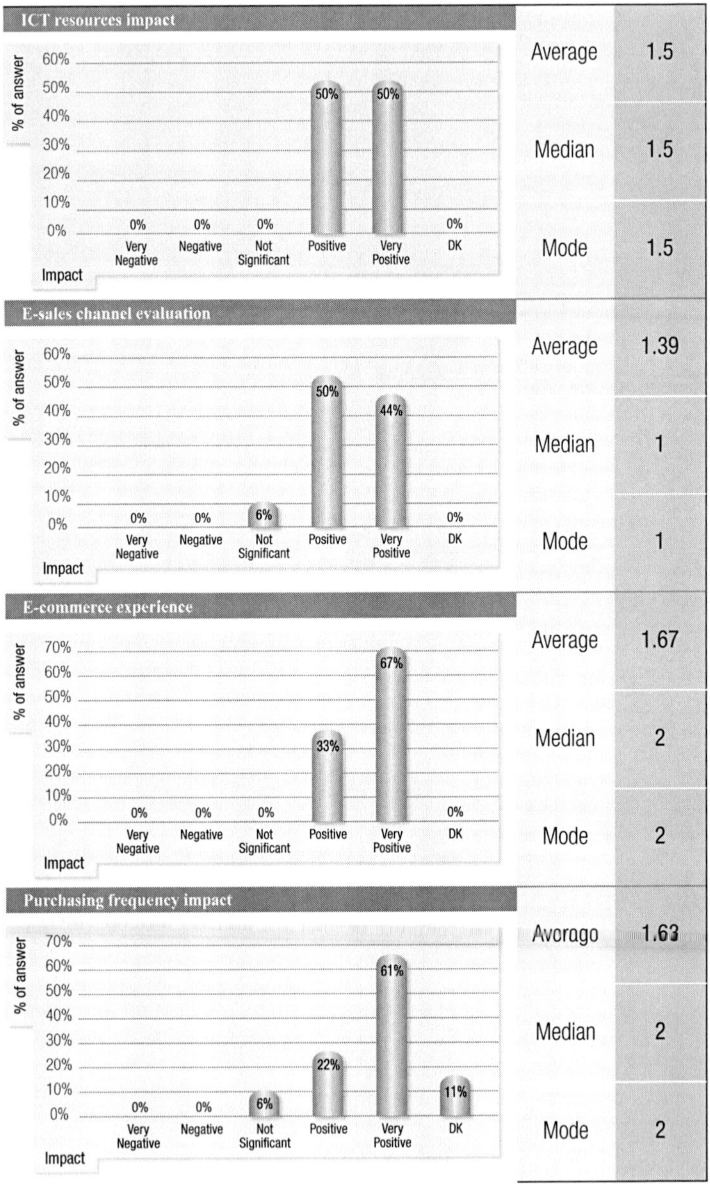

Figure 4-3 Customer characteristics impact on e-commerce customer propensity

3.3. Customer characteristics

The analysis of customer characteristics, provided on the basis of the Delphi results, is in compliance with previous theoretical findings. All success factors, characterizing customer's propensity to adopt e-purchasing, have a positive influence. Two factors, e-commerce experience and purchasing frequency, are considered as the main drivers of customer behavior, both having a very positive impact. The factors ICT resources and especially e-sales channel evaluation are considered by the experts as less important and are characterized by just a positive impact, as can be seen in Figure 4-3.

3.4. Purchasing process modifications

The use of a Delphi study allows researchers to delve deeper into the details to classify the impact of purchasing process modifications. Three different aspects have been considered, as shown in Figure 4-4. The most important one, characterized by a very positive impact, is clearly process improvement, followed by back-office integration and purchasing price reduction, both having a positive impact. The relative importance of back-office integration seems the most variable, assuming quite often a non significant or a very positive impact, according to the specific market environment and to the considered breadth of the value creation definition, thus to the sophistication of the e-commerce solution (Chopra et al. 2001).

3.5. Brand perception

As expected, brand reputation and brand awareness have a positive impact, with the former having a stronger effect. Distance seems to act as a negative effect; however, the wide range of expert answers, illustrated in Figure 4-5, suggests further analysis is required before definitively assigning its impact.

4. Development rule-based decision support system

The utility of rule-based DSS in the field of e-commerce has already been demonstrated by Zhou et al. (2004), which points out the broad managerial implications of the discovered rules. These rules can be directly used, even if qualitative, to support business strategic planning and decision making of pure e-commerce and multi-channel retailers. A similar objective is pursued by the developed DSS that can classify the success of an e-strategy in terms of sales turnover increase rate and of maximum turnover, depending on the targeted customers, the sold products and the adopted e-sales channel. The DSS is formalized through a series of IF… THEN rules dealing with linguistic variables.

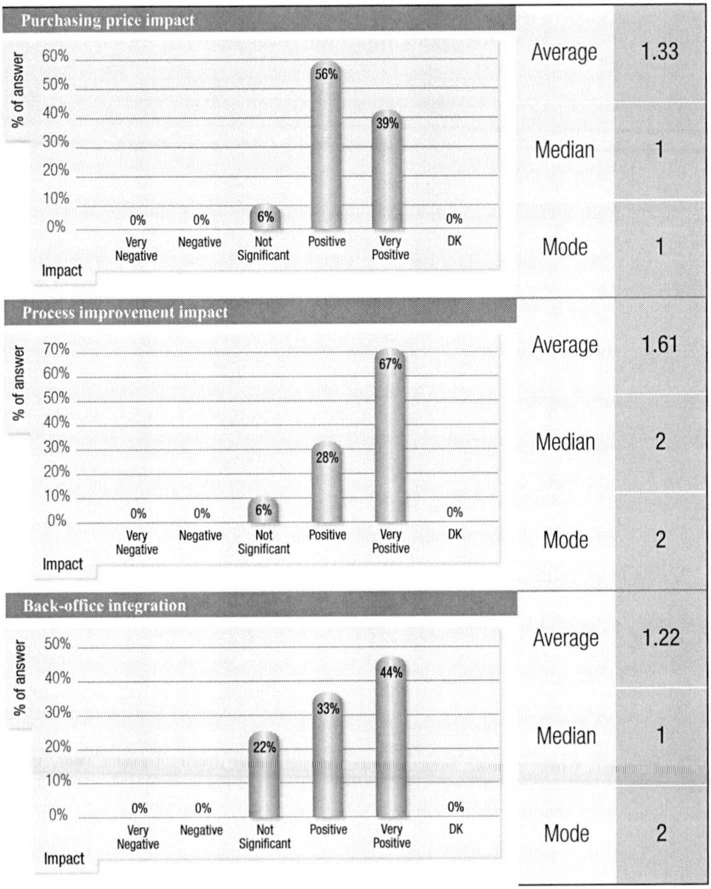

Figure 4-4 Purchasing process modification impact on e-commerce competitive advantage

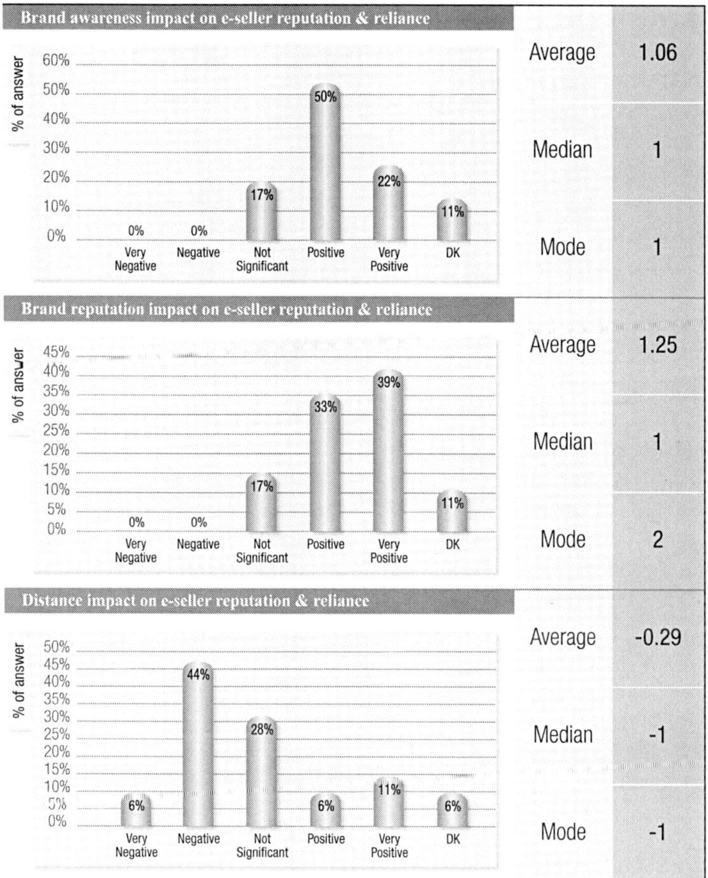

Figure 4-5 Brand perception related success factors impact on e-seller reputation & reliance

The choice of linguistic variables, measured through qualitative notations (e.g. low, medium, high), is justified by the following elements:

- The qualitative and subjective nature of many of the factors that are linked to customer perception;
- The simplicity for company management of providing qualitative estimations rather than gathering quantitative data that are particularly difficult to obtain for activities such as e-commerce that are still in their infancy.

In order to keep the sets of rules to an understandable and manageable size, the DSS data are structured into three categories (e-commerce success factors, aggregated factors, output variables) as shown in Figure 4-6. For simplicity reasons, in this work the proposed DSS is illustrated by considering a limited number of levels for the linguistic variables. More specifically, three levels are used for describing the e-commerce success factors (low, medium, high), while five levels are used for the aggregated factors and the output variables (very low, low, medium, high, very high).

4.1. DSS output variables

The DSS outputs (Saturation level and Speed of adoption), shown on the right hand side of Figure 4-6, provide an appropriate description of a typical e-commerce evolution pattern. These variables have been chosen because they provide an effective modeling of the company e-sales evolution through the application of the concepts of DOI theory. The theoretical relevance of the DSS outputs is proven by their previous successful application to ICT and e-commerce adoption descriptions (Rai et al. 1998; Samaddar et al. 2002; Teng et al. 2002). Furthermore, they enrich the DSS with quantitative data. In fact, quantitative estimations can be associated to the linguistic values of Saturation level and Speed of adoption. They are obtained by applying nonlinear mathematical diffusion models, such as Bass (Teng et al. 2002; Ure 2002; Wright et al. 1997), Gompertz (Rai et al. 1998; Samaddar et al. 2002) and Logistic (Santarelli and D'Altri 2001; Skjevdal and Vik 2004) to e-commerce historical data.

4.2. Rule sets for aggregated factors

The e-commerce success factors, defined in section 2, appear on the left hand side of Figure 4.6. The aggregated factors called *Product*, *Customer*, *Process* and *Brand* are obtained by combining the e-commerce success factors, according to the results of the Delphi study (section 3). The aggregated factor *Product* characterizes the product suitability for e-purchasing, *Customer* describes the customer propensity to adopt e-purchasing, *Process* estimates the impact of purchasing process modifications and *Brand* represents brand awareness and reputation as well as the distance impact on the customer's perceived risk (used only when considering new potential customers). The aggregated factors appear in the central part of Figure 4-6. Each set of rules is constructed starting from the identification of the direction (positive or negative) and the magnitude of the influence of each e-commerce success factor.

As an example, in the set of rules leading to the linguistic values of the aggregated factor *Customer* all of the four e-commerce success factors have a positive influence. The most important factors are e-commerce experience and purchasing frequency, both with a very positive impact. ICT resources and e-sales channel evaluation are considered less important, the latter having only a positive impact. This set of rules, defining the values of the aggregated factor *Customer*, results in a full factorial combination of the levels of the four inputs (3^4=81 rules) described in detail in Table 4-2.

ICT	E-exp	E-SC	Freq	Cus	ICT	E-exp	E-SC	Freq	Cus	ICT	E-exp	E-SC	Freq	Cus
L	L	L	L	VL	M	L	L	L	VL	H	L	L	L	L
L	L	L	M	L	M	L	L	M	L	H	L	L	M	L
L	L	L	H	L	M	L	L	H	M	H	L	L	H	M
L	L	M	L	VL	M	L	M	L	L	H	L	M	L	L
L	L	M	M	L	M	L	M	M	L	H	L	M	M	M
L	L	M	H	M	M	L	M	H	M	H	L	M	H	M
L	L	H	L	L	M	L	H	L	L	H	L	H	L	L
L	L	H	M	L	M	L	H	M	M	H	L	H	M	M
L	L	H	H	M	M	L	H	H	M	H	L	H	H	H
L	M	L	L	L	M	M	L	L	L	H	M	L	L	L
L	M	L	M	L	M	M	L	M	M	H	M	L	M	M
L	M	L	H	M	M	M	L	H	M	H	M	L	H	H
L	M	M	L	L	M	M	M	L	L	H	M	M	L	M
L	M	M	M	M	M	M	M	M	M	H	M	M	M	M
L	M	M	H	M	M	M	M	H	H	H	M	M	H	H
L	M	H	L	L	M	M	H	L	M	H	M	H	L	M
L	M	H	M	M	M	M	H	M	M	H	M	H	M	H
L	M	H	H	H	M	M	H	H	H	H	M	H	H	H
L	H	L	L	L	M	H	L	L	M	H	H	L	L	M
L	H	L	M	M	M	H	L	M	M	H	H	L	M	H
L	H	L	H	H	M	H	L	H	H	H	H	L	H	H
L	H	M	L	M	M	H	M	L	M	H	H	M	L	M
L	H	M	M	M	M	H	M	M	H	H	H	M	M	H
L	H	M	H	H	M	H	M	H	H	H	H	M	H	VH
L	H	H	L	M	M	H	H	L	M	H	H	H	L	H
L	H	H	M	H	M	H	H	M	H	H	H	H	M	H
L	H	H	H	H	M	H	H	H	VH	H	H	H	H	VH

INPUT (3 levels) ICT = ICT resources; E-exp = e-commerce experience; E-SC = e-sales channel evaluation;
Freq = purchasing frequency
OUTPUT (5 levels) Cus = customer propensity to adopt e-purchasing
VL = very low; L = low; M = medium; H = high; VH = very high

Table 4-2 DSS rules for aggregated factor Customer

4.3. Rule sets for output variables

The set of rules linking the aggregated factors to the output variable are also elaborated using the results of the first round of the Delphi study. In these sets of rules the aggregated factors should all have a positive influence. For this reason, in this section of the Delphi questionnaire the experts are asked to use a different notation for describing their impact: (VI) very important, (I) important, (SI) somewhat important, (SNI) somewhat not important, (ANI) absolutely not important, (DK) do not know.

For customers belonging to the current customer base, only three aggregated factors are considered for the determination of the output variables, specifically *Product*, *Customer* and *Process*. On the other hand, considering that the perceived risk for new potential customers is clearly higher than for customers that already know the supplier and its products, the aggregated factor *Brand* is also used for elaborating the set of rules regarding new customers.

Process is the most important attribute for both Saturation level and Speed of adoption. This can be explained by its impact on perceived usefulness and its capacity to describe the purchasing company's long-term benefits of e-sales channels utilization. Thus, on the basis of the preliminary Delphi results (Figure 4-7 and Figure 4-8) a very positive impact is assigned to *Process*. Furthermore, the analysis of the Delphi results demonstrates that this is the attribute for which the greatest level of convergence is obtained, especially in the case of the prediction of the Saturation level. The absence of a sufficient degree of convergence for the remaining three aggregated factors at this stage of the Delphi study does not hinder the possibility of deriving useful information from the expert answers already collected. *Customer* appears to be the second most relevant attribute, having an impact slightly above important. Just below important are the impacts of *Brand* and *Product*; however, especially for the latter it is difficult to establish what will be the final outcome of the Delphi study. At this stage of the work all of the aggregated factors appear to have a significant impact on e-sales evolution. The following is a first tentative ranking, according to decreasing value of importance, of the four factors: *Process* (VI), *Customer* (I), *Brand* (I) and *Product* (I). Even if the rating of the aggregated factors obtained while analyzing Saturation level are slightly different from those obtained in the case of Speed of adoption, the same ranking applies to the rules defining both output variables. A more detailed classification of the importance of the aggregated factors will be available at the end of the Delphi study, however they are expected to be only slightly different than the current ones due to the relatively high degree of convergence already obtained.

DSS DELPHI 1st round

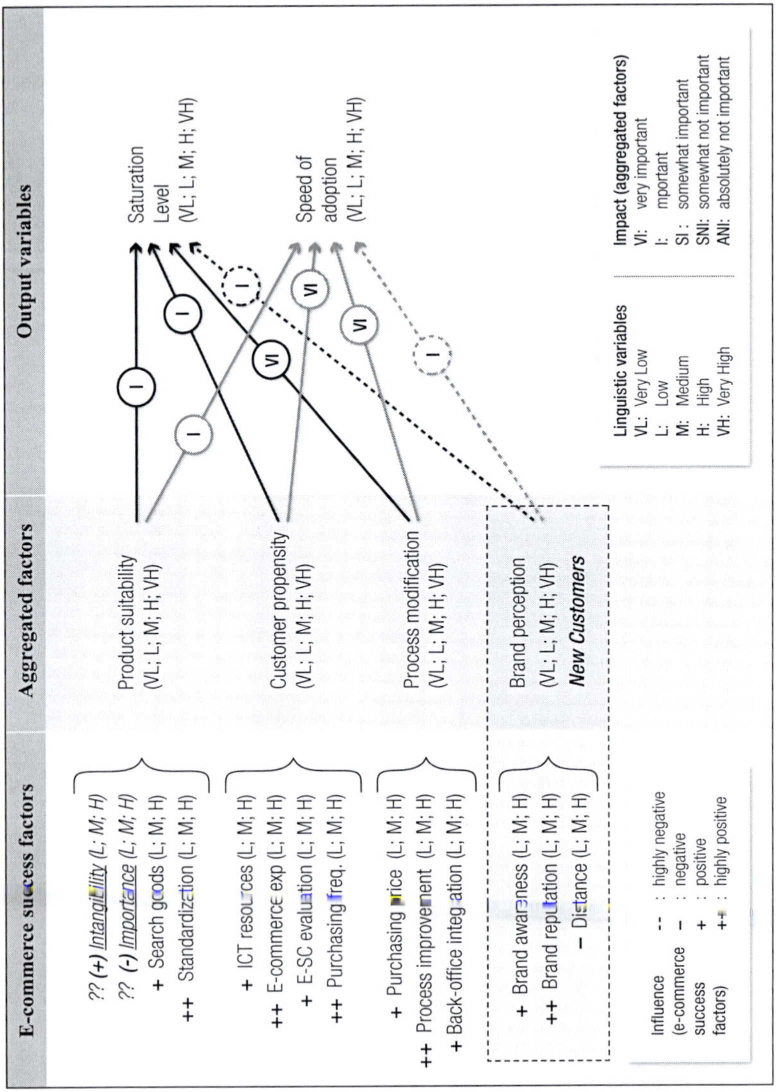

Figure 4-6 Rule-based decision support system structure

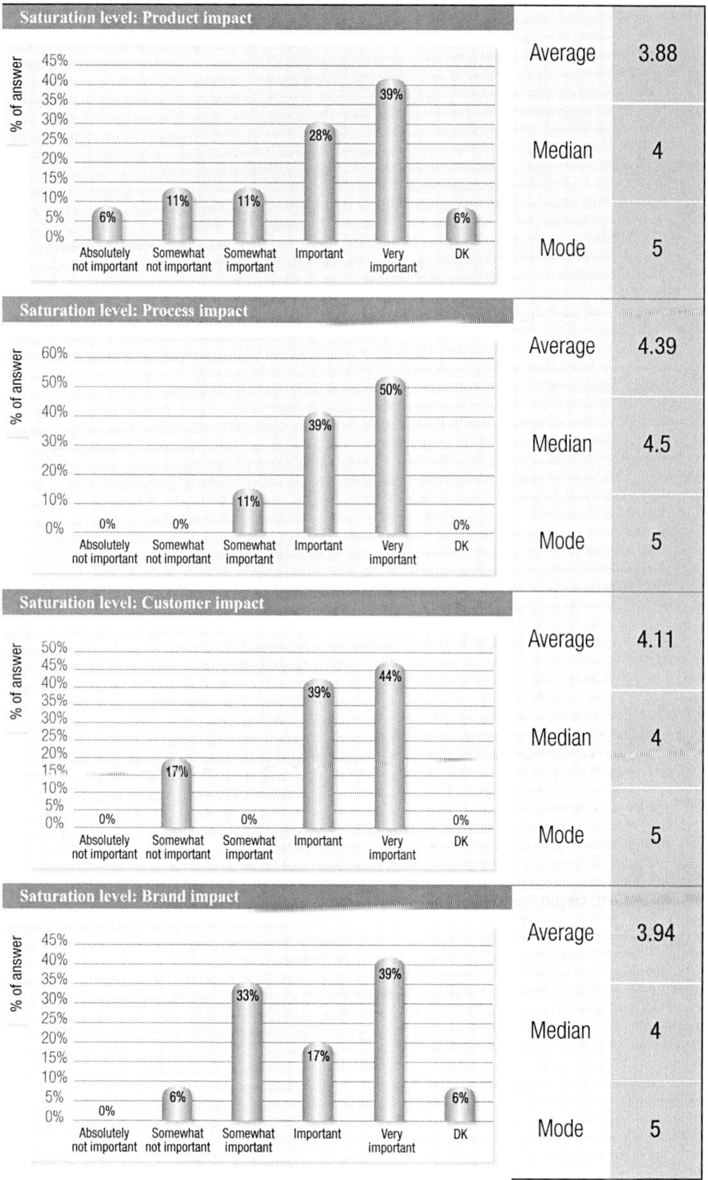

Figure 4-7 Aggregated factors impact on e-commerce saturation level

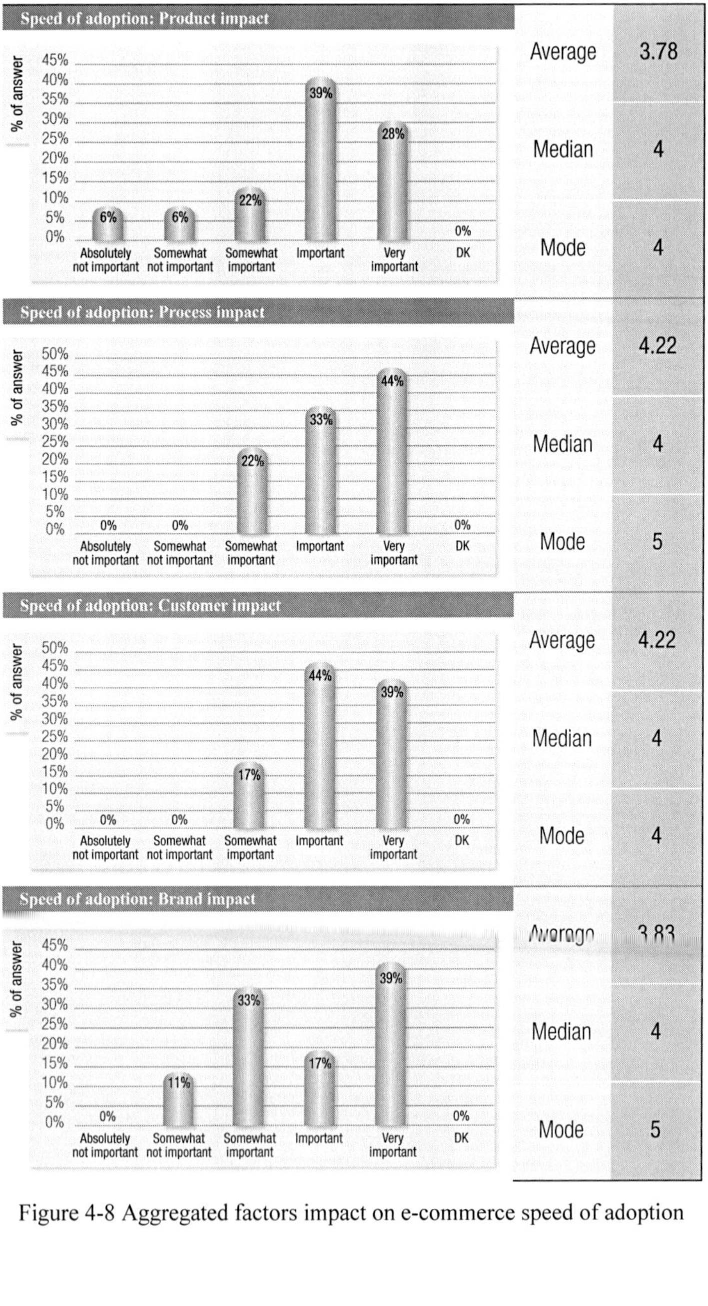

Figure 4-8 Aggregated factors impact on e-commerce speed of adoption

Conclusion

This chapter presents a complete framework supporting the identification and the qualitative description of the main e-commerce success factors, which characterize a specific company within a particular industrial sector. On the basis of a literature review, the success factors are identified and arranged according to four dimensions: product features, customer characteristics, process modifications and brand perception. The four considered dimensions expand the findings of previous frameworks and ensure a better understanding of the company's environment.

A formalized relationship is established between the qualitative description of the company environment, provided by the linguistic values of the e-commerce success factors, and that of the e-sales evolution pattern. This relationship is expressed through the DSS rules, which can be considered as a first attempt to predict the evolution of e-sales and to explain the factors influencing it. The DSS rules are based on the analysis of the reviewed literature and are further validated and complemented relying upon the findings of the preliminary results of a Delphi study involving 18 experts. The use of linguistic values in the DSS rules facilitates the assessment by the company decision makers of the impacts of the market environment and of the implemented e-strategy, and therefore supports an effective application of the proposed DSS by the end users. Moreover, the latter is facilitated by a software module that, once specified the values of the e-commerce success factors, can automatically estimate the qualitative value of aggregated factors and DSS output. The developed DSS tool is part of a more comprehensive e-sales modeling framework, which aims at complementing the qualitative description of e-commerce evolution by adding quantitative information. This completely specifies the e-sales dynamics in terms of sold quantities, through the application of a suitable DOI mathematical model over a specified time horizon.

The obtained results are in agreement with the previous literature. The qualitative description provided by the rule-based DSS can be further improved by integrating results from future research. This will be achieved by relying upon expert opinions, such as those already collected through the Delphi study as well as through case study analysis of companies involved in e-commerce. In particular, the investigation of case studies will provide a clear understanding of the impact of factors for which a convergence of expert opinions seems impossible.

CHAPTER FIVE

SMEs' USE OF WEB-BASED INTERORGANIZATIONAL INFORMATION SYSTEMS TO SHARE INVENTORY INFORMATION

ROBERT PELLERIN AND PIERRE HADAYA

Introduction

Supply chain collaboration is defined as two or more companies sharing responsibility for exchanging common planning, management, execution, and performance measurement information (Anthony 2000). The fundamental rationale behind the concept is that by pooling their resources, collaborative supply chain partners can perform better than they could if each firm operated individually (Lambert et al. 1999). Inventory and cost savings (Sabath and Fontanella 2002; Stank et al. 1999), better demand planning (McCarthy and Golicic 2002), increased operational flexibility to cope with uncertain demand (Fisher 1997; Lee et al. 1997), increased customer loyalty (Sabath and Fontanella 2002), and the development of new skills and competencies (Verespej 2005) are just some of the benefits firms expect from supply chain collaboration.

Supply chain collaboration can be achieved in different ways, including methods such as collaborative planning, forecasting and replenishment (CPFR) and vendor-managed inventory (VMI), but collaborating electronically has become a common way of initiating or improving supplier-buyer relationships. Facilitated by Web-based tools and other interorganizational information systems (IOISs) such as B2B e-commerce tools, the term e-collaboration is now used to describe relationships that go beyond simple buy-and-sell transactions (Johnson and Whang 2002). Today, Web-based IOISs play a crucial role in the evolution of supply chain relationships as they are able to support a number of collaboration processes ranging from direct procurement, replenishment, and delivery and design, to more strategic processes such as capacity planning (Cassivi 2006).

Despite managers' and researchers' awareness of the value of e-collaboration (Min et al. 2005; Munkvold and Zigurs 2005), empirical studies measuring the extent of e-collaboration within supply chain networks show mixed results. While studies focusing on organized networks led by major system integrators (original equipment manufacturers, or OEMs) show significant levels of integration and collaboration (Cassivi et al. 2004; Cassivi 2006), other studies have found that only a few companies are engaged at the level of integration that the concept of collaboration suggests (Fawcett and Magnan 2004). Moreover, few studies address the views of SMEs involved in various and sometimes unstructured supply chain networks.

Recognizing the importance of SMEs to national economies, it therefore seems important to identify the factors that incite manufacturing SMEs to collaborate electronically. More specifically, we propose to study one of the key dimensions of supply chain collaboration: information sharing (Simatupang and Sridharan 2005). More than in traditional supply chains, information sharing between firms is anchored in the use of electronic commerce and information technologies. This new kind of temporary interorganizational system provides great opportunities for manufacturing SMEs to establish or to extend their activities in international markets. By taking advantage of the technical capabilities of the Internet, manufacturing SMEs that are members of virtual enterprises may be able to skip the lengthy, incremental process generally required to participate in global markets, as they can improve communication with foreign buyers and partners, gain access to up-to-date international marketing information, and undertake global sales promotion online (Hamill and Gregory 1997; Ho et al. 2003). The Internet can also provide a low-cost "gateway" to international markets and overcome many of the barriers to internationalization that SMEs commonly face (Moen et al. 2004; Quelch and Klein 1996).

This chapter's objective is to measure the influence of various determinants on manufacturing firms' intent to use Web-based interorganizational information systems to share inventory information with their key customers. The remainder of the chapter is organized as follows. First, we present a classification of Web-based interorganizational information systems. Then, the research model and hypotheses are exposed with the relevant literature regarding e-commerce strategies and collaboration. Next, the research methodology is explained. Then, our research results are presented and discussed. Finally, the paper will conclude with the research limitations and the prospects for future research.

1. Classification of interorganizational information systems

The term IOIS was first proposed in the early 1980s, when Barrett and Konsynski (1982) used it to refer to an automated information system shared by two or more organizations. IOISs are computer networks that support information exchanges across organizational boundaries (Choudhury 1997) and enable the electronic integration of business transactions and collaborative processes carried out by two or more organizations. Electronic data interchange (EDI) is probably the most commonly used technology allowing the exchange of information between business partners. However, in today's digital economy, more and more firms are turning to Web-based approaches to support their interorganizational activities. As Elgarah et al. (2005) point out, "this migration reflects a movement away from a dyadic approach in data exchange, to more flexible cost-effective approaches that capitalize on many-to-many relationships" (p. 8).

Although all IOISs provide communication benefits, they may differ in their ability to provide superior integration and brokerage ability (Choudhury 1997; Malone et al. 1987). Thus, some IOISs are primarily adopted to enable the electronic integration of business transactions between a firm and a large number of its trading partners, while others are more appropriate to enable the electronic integration of collaborative processes (through information sharing) between a few supply chain partners. This large variability in terms of IOIS functionalities has led researchers to propose numerous classification frameworks (Barrett and Konsynski 1982; Hadaya 2004; Hong 2002; Johnston and Vitale 1988; Kumar and van Dissel 1996; Malone et al. 1987; Samaddar et al. 2006). For example, Kumar and van Dissel's (1996) typology, which characterizes IOISs along the dimension of interdependency in interfirm relationships, classifies them into three types: (1) pooled information resource IOISs that permit the sharing of common IS/IT resources;

(2) value/supply chain IOISs that support specific customer-supplier relationships; and (3) networked IOISs that operationalize and implement reciprocal interdependencies between organizations. Choudhury's (1997) typology, however, comprises electronic dyads (including the special case of electronic monopolies when applied to a single product) and multilateral IOISs. Electronic dyads support bilateral communication involving one buyer (seller) and a few sellers (buyers) while multilateral IOISs allow a firm to communicate with a large number of trading partners over a single interorganizational link.

In the particular context of Business-to-Business (B2B) internet commerce, we recognize six types of Web-based IOISs that are commonly used to support interorganizational processes (adapted from Hadaya 2004): (1) data interchange; (2) sell-side solution; (3) extranet; (4) buy-side solution; (5) public electronic marketplace, and (6) private trading exchanges (PTX). Evidently, the objective and characteristics vary from one Web-based IOIS to the next, as illustrated in Table 5-1. By studying the above mentioned and other IOIS classification schemes, one sees that firms need to adopt and assimilate different kinds of IOISs to support the different types of buyer-seller relationships they maintain with their pool of suppliers and customers (Saeed et al. 2005) and address the top-priority performance improvements required by the supply chain network within which they operate (Da Silveira and Cagliano 2006).

	Data interchange	Sell-side solution	Extranet	Buy-side solution	Electronic marketplace	Private trading exchange
Objectives	Inter-organizational, computer-to-computer exchange of structured information in a non-proprietary machine-processable format	Allows a firm to centralize all the information regarding its products/services on a single electronic platform in order for them to be accessible, generally via an electronic catalogue, by its customers (Net Market Makers, 1999)	A private network that uses Internet protocols, network connectivity, and possibly the public telecommunication system to securely share part of an organization's information or operations with suppliers, vendors, partners, customers or other businesses. An extranet can be viewed as part of a company's Intranet that is extended to users outside the company	Centralizes all the information regarding the products/services of suppliers on a single platform owned and operated by a buyer, in order for this information to be accessible by all the employees of the organization via an electronic catalogue, an ERP, legacy system, etc. (Net Market Makers, 1999	An intermediary that allows buyers and sellers to meet on an electronic platform in order to exchange information about products/services (price, specifica-tions, etc.), conduct transactions online and adhere to other value-added services (settlement, distribution, integration, etc.) offered by the intermediary (Hadaya, 2006)	Allows a prime contractor to conduct electronic transactions and collaborate with its customers and suppliers on a single electronic platform (Bermudez, 2001)

Software applications	Each firm involved uses its own software package, e-collaboration tool, legacy systems, etc.	Web applications (owned by the administrator of the Web-based IOIS) accessible via a thin client (e.g. browser)				
Actors involved	A firm and one or many of its suppliers and/or one or many of its customers	A firm and its customers	A firm and its customers and/or suppliers	A firm and its suppliers	An intermediary with buyers and sellers	A prime contractor with its suppliers and customers
Administrator	The prime contractor (buyer or seller)	The seller	The prime contractor (buyer or seller)	The buyer	An intermediary (neutral proprietary or consortium)	The prime contractor (buyer and seller)
Type of data exchanged	Transactional and collaborative	Transactional and collaborative	Transactional and collaborative	Transactional and collaborative	Transactional (mostly) and collaborative	Transactional and collaborative
Benefits	Decreases transaction and coordination costs Strengthens ties and encourages long term relationships	Lowers the costs of sales Creates an online storefront open 24 hours a day	Strengthen relationships with existing partners Rapid and inexpensive deployment Easy to use	Strengthen relation-ships with existing partners Allows corporate procurement organizations to combine multiple supplier catalogues into a universal enterprise catalogue and to deploy self-service requisition-ing and order processing to the user desktop	Low technological entry barrier Reduces buyers' search costs by consolidating sellers and products on a single electronic platform Exposes the sellers to a larger market potential	Prime contractor: centralizes all business processes on the same internal platform and facilitates interactions, transactions and collaboration with customers and suppliers. Business partners: diminishes investments risk by getting access to electronic commerce applications in ASP format.
Example	Data exchange between Intel and its suppliers	An SMEs Web site	Adaptec's Extranet used to collaborate with its key wafer fabricators and assemblers	Raytheon's TRADE'ex Procurement solution	Chemconnect	Cisco's and Dell's PTX

Table 5-1 Five models of Web-based IOISs

2. Research framework

A number of authors have attempted to identify several variables as possible determinants of a firm's adoption of information technology. According to Fichman (2000), these determinants can be grouped into three categories: (1) those pertaining to the technologies and their diffusion contexts, including Rogers' (1995) attributes of innovations and the innovation characteristics identified by Tornatzky and Klein (1982) and others; (2) those pertaining to organizations and their adoption contexts, including firms' structural characteristics such as centralization and formalization (Zmud 1982); and (3) those pertaining to the combination of technology and organization, including several process models used to guide innovation implementation (Brynjolfsson et al. 1997).

However, some authors argue that a unifying theory might be inappropriate due to the fundamental differences between the different types of innovations (Downs and Mohr 1976; Fichman and Kemerer 1993). Also, no prior empirical study has yet attempted to measure the influence of various determinants on SME manufacturing firms' intent to use Web-based IOISs to share inventory information with their key customers. Therefore, we have limited our study to a set of variables related to the technology and to the business relationships (see Figure 5-1) which are described in the following sub-sections.

2.1 Determinant related to technology: organizational readiness

Organizational readiness is a measure of the technical and financial resources that are prerequisites for the adoption of IOISs (Swatman and Swatman 1991). Studies have demonstrated that technological characteristics (e.g., IT infrastructure and IT capabilities) can encourage or hinder the adoption of IOISs (Premkumar and Ramamurthy 1995). Organizational readiness, in the form of IS capabilities, is also required to support CPFR initiatives (Stank et al. 1999) or other methods adopted by neighboring partners in a supply chain that share inventory information. Other studies have also shown that adequate financial resources increase the success of IOIS adoption (Saunders and Clark 1992). Some researchers have also found that organizational readiness positively affects firms' adoption of different types of IOISs, such as EDI (Iacovou et al. 1995) and Web-based IOISs (Chang and Chen 2005). Finally, organizational readiness has also been identified in previous studies as one of the main factors that influence the adoption of IOIS by SMEs (Grandon and Pearson 2004; Mackay et al. 2004; Mehrtens et al. 2001) as SMEs often lack the financial and non-financial resources as well as the knowledge to implement sophisticated technologies (Cragg and King 1993; Mehrtens et al. 2001).

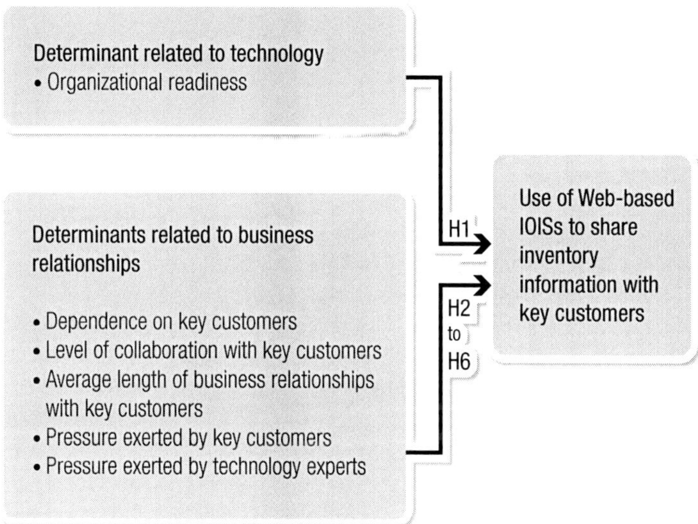

Figure 5-1 Conceptual model

These arguments lead to our first hypothesis:

Hypothesis 1: A manufacturing SME's organizational readiness will be positively related to its use of Web-based IOISs to share inventory information with its key customers.

2.2 Determinant-related business relationships

The determinants related to business relationships seem to be the ones which exert the most powerful influence on the adoption of innovations which impact both a firm and its business partners (Fichman 2000; Prescott and Conger 1995), as is the case for collaborative Web-based IOISs. Five determinants corresponding to the characteristics of a manufacturing firm's business relationships may influence a company's use of Web-based IOISs to share inventory information with its key customers: its dependency on its key customers, its level of collaboration with its key customers, the average length of business relationships with its key customers, the pressure it undergoes from its key customers, and the pressure exerted by technology experts.

Dependency can be defined as a firm's need to maintain an exchange relationship with another company in order to fulfill some of its objectives (Frazier and Rody 1991; Ganesan 1994). There is a positive relationship between a firm's dependency on another firm and its level of coordination with the latter (Lonsdale 2001; Malone and Crowston 1994; Williamson 1975). Some authors have demonstrated that a firm's level of vertical coordination with its business partners is positively linked to the adoption of information technologies (Gatignon and Robertson 1989).

Other researchers have also demonstrated that dependency on their suppliers often forces manufacturing firms to use IOISs to collaborate with the latter in order to safeguard against opportunistic behaviors that might undermine this key relationship (Christy and Grout 1994; Kersten et al. 2004; Léger et al. 2006). This influence may be stronger for SMEs, because their business volume with some customers may be critical to their survival. On the basis of these arguments, we may infer that a manufacturing SME's dependency on its key customers will influence its use of Web-based IOISs to share inventory information with them.

Based on these arguments, we formulated our second hypothesis:

Hypothesis 2: *A manufacturing SME's dependency on its key customers positively influences its use of Web-based IOISs to share inventory information with those key customers.*

Information sharing is at the heart of collaboration (Min et al. 2005). And, according to Marquez et al. (2004), there is a broad consensus that information systems integration is essential to efficiently support information sharing between supply chain partners. Indeed, IOISs are essential to efficiently support the VMI and CPFR methods of exchanging inventory information and improving supply chain performance (Chen 1999; Towill et al. 1992; Wikner et al. 1991).

These arguments gave rise to our third hypothesis:

Hypothesis 3: *A manufacturing SME's level of collaboration with its key customers positively influences its use of Web-based IOISs to share inventory information with those key customers.*

As Mentzer et al. (2001) stated, the goal of supply chain management is for member organizations to work together in close, long-term relationships to increase the competitive advantage of the supply chain as a whole. The partnering relationships that ensue are thus characterized by a high level of trust, a long-term relationship orientation, intensive information exchange, and a high level of mutual cooperation (Lewin and Johnson 1997). According to Hunt et al. (2006), the decision to adopt an IOIS is not a unilateral one and its successful adoption requires the existence of a strong relationship among the firms involved. These arguments are consistent with Wu et al.'s (2004) findings demonstrating that long-term relationships, through commitment, enhance the integration of the supply chain management business process. Also, firms involved in long term relationships with their key partners will be more willing to adopt VMI and CPFR methods as these inter-enterprise initiatives generally require the development of specific assets (Cassivi 2006).

These arguments lead to the fourth hypothesis:

Hypothesis 4: *A manufacturing SME's average length of business relationship with its key customers positively influences its use of Web-based IOISs to share inventory information with those key customers.*

A firm that undergoes pressure from its business partners – such as customers, suppliers, investors, and technology providers – may be compelled to initiate and implement certain practices (Bower 1996;

Christensen and Foster 1986). This pressure may be more important for SMEs (Hart and Saunders 1997) especially when the innovation is an interdependent technology, such as an IOIS (Bensaou and Venkatraman 1996; Grover 1993; Iacovou et al. 1995; Premkumar and Ramamurthy 1995; Reekers and Smithson 1994; Riggins and Mukhopadyay 1994) and Internet-based tools that support the exchange of inventory information among supply chain partners (Disney and Towill 2003; Saeed et al. 2005). Two variables are included in our research model to assess the pressure exerted by key customers and technology experts on manufacturing firms.

Based on all the arguments discussed above, we made the following hypotheses:

Hypothesis 5: *The pressure a manufacturing SME experiences from its key customers will be positively related to its use of Web-based IOISs to share inventory information with those key customers.*

Hypothesis 6: *The pressure a manufacturing SME experiences from technology experts will be positively related to its use of Web-based IOISs to share inventory information with its key customers.*

3 Research methodology

All data were collected by means of an electronic questionnaire. Although this method may limit our panel, and lower our response rate, it offers numerous advantages compared to traditional questionnaires, such as saving time and money (Dillman 2000; Weible and Wallace 1998) and ensuring data integrity (Mann and Stewart 2000).

A systematic sample was derived from an up-to-date list of manufacturing firms in one Canadian province obtained from a firm that specializes in Internet-based direct marketing. An e-mail was sent out to around 2,200 sales managers in manufacturing SMEs, explaining the research subject and providing a hyperlink to the electronic survey. SMEs in the context of this paper are defined according to Statistics Canada's definition: firms employing fewer than 500 full-time equivalent workers.

In order to obtain the highest response rate and encourage respondents to respond to the whole survey, a personalized benchmark report was provided to those who took the time to participate in the electronic survey. A total of 240 questionnaires were properly completed. No significant differences (goodness of fit tests) were found between respondents and non-respondents with respect to firm size.

The survey instrument (presented in Appendix A) comprised both observable variables (e.g., dependency on key customers and average length of business relationships with key customers) and latent variables (e.g., organizational readiness and the level of collaboration with key customers).

The *organizational readiness* construct measures the extent to which manufacturing firms have the necessary predisposition to use Web-based IOISs to share inventory information with their key customers. Thus, this variable measures, on a 7-point Likert scale where 1 = "completely disagree" and 7 = "completely agree," the extent to which manufacturing firms have (1) the necessary management support (Grandon and Pearson 2004); (2) the necessary financial resources (Grandon and Pearson 2004); (3) staff members willing to change the way they work; (4) knowledgeable IT staff (Mehrtens et al., 2001); (5) knowledgeable non-IT staff (Mehrtens et al. 2001); (6) adequate IT infrastructure (Premkumar and Roberts 1999); and (7) an adequate level of systems integration with existing IS to use Web-based IOISs (Grandon and Pearson 2004; Premkumar and Ramamurthy 1995).

Sheppard and Sherman's (1998) operationalization is used to measure manufacturing firms' dependency on key customers: the nature of the relationship is dependent (unilateral) and the intensity is deep. Hence, a firm that has a limited number of customers that represents 75 percent or more of its procurement is categorized as dependent.

The *level of collaboration with key customers* construct measures the extent to which manufacturing firms participate in collaborative planning and take joint actions with their key customers. These two items are measured on a 7-point Likert scale where 1 = "not at all" and 7 = "to a great extent."

The number of months is used to measure the *average length of business relationships with key customers*. The *pressure exerted by key customers* and *use of Web-based IOISs to share inventory information with key customers* measure respectively the extent to which manufacturing firms are influenced by their key customers and the extent to which they use Web-based to share inventory information with those key suppliers.

The *pressure exerted by technology experts* construct gauges the extent to which SMEs are influenced by consultants and integrators. These two items are measured on a 7-point Likert scale where 1 = "not at all" and 7 = "to a great extent."

To obtain a preliminary assessment of the validity of the research construct, twenty manufacturing firms participated in a pre-test of the survey instruments. Comments from the subjects resulted in minor changes to survey questions.

4 Analytical procedure

Data analysis was carried out using a two-stage methodology. The first measurement model comprised the first three constructs: organizational readiness, level of collaboration with key customers and pressure exerted by technology experts. As a second step, multivariate data analyses were conducted to assess the influence of the determinants on the use of Web-based IOISs to share inventory information with key customers. Since a significant number of firms – 106 to be precise – indicated that they did not use Web-based IOISs to share inventory information with key customers, and thus gave a zero value to the variable, the Tobit model was deemed more appropriate than the conventional regression model to assess the influence of the determinants on the use of Web-based IOISs to share inventory information with key customers, given that it takes into account the truncated distribution of the dependent variable (Damsgaard and Lyytinen 1996; Greene 1997). Indeed, the Tobit model, devised by Tobin (1958), assumes that the dependent variable has a number of its values clustered at a limiting value, usually zero. The stochastic model underlying Tobit may be expressed by the following relationship (McDonald and Moffit 1980):

$$
\begin{aligned}
y_t &= X_t\beta + u_t && \text{if } X_t\beta + u_t > 0 \\
&= 0 && \text{if } X_t\beta + u_t \leq 0
\end{aligned}
$$

$t = 1,2,3,\ldots,N.$

where:

N is the number of observations;

y_t is the dependent variable;

β is a vector of unknown coefficients; and
u_t is an independently distributed error term assumed to be normal with zero mean and constant variance σ^2.

The three constructs of the research model were subject to two confirmatory factor analysis (CFA) using LISREL for Windows v8.12a. The validity of the constructs was assessed in terms of internal consistency and discriminant validity. The internal consistency of each dimension is assessed by computing the Cronbach's alpha (Hair et al. 1998). Table 5-2 shows that all Cronbach's alpha exceed the recommended 0.70 threshold (Nunnally 1978).

Construct	Number of items	Cronbach's alpha
Organizational readiness	7	0.91
Level of collaboration with key customers	2	0.83
Pressure exerted by technology experts	2	0.77

Table 5-2 Internal consistency

Similarly, discriminant validity is defined as the degree of uniqueness achieved from item measures in defining a latent construct (Gefen 2003). The variables are distinct since the correlations between all pairs of variables constructs were below the 0.8 threshold proposed by Venkatraman (1989) (see Table 5-3). In summary, our confirmatory analysis shows strong evidence of internal consistency and discriminant validity of the model.

Construct	(1)	(2)	(3)	(4)	(5)	(6)
(1) Readiness	1.00					
(2) Dependency on key customers	0.07	1.00				
(3) Level of collaboration with key customers	0.13**	0.08	1.00			
(4) Average length of business relationships with key customers	0.13	0.16**	0.06	1.00		
(5) Pressure exerted by key customers	0.10*	0.06	0.42****	0.11*	1.00	
(6) Pressure exerted by technology experts	0.46****	0.01	0.19***	0.03	0.3****	1.00

Table 5-3 Intercorrelation matrix[1]

[1] p = level of two-tailed significance based on a chi-square distribution where * p < .10, ** p < .05, *** p < .01, **** p < .001

5 Results and discussion

The data collected from the 240 manufacturing firms were compiled and analyzed with SAS v. 8.2 (TS2M0) and SPSS for Windows (vs 15.0). The results of the Tobit regression are presented in Table 5-4.

Variables	ß	Wald	p[2]
Organizational readiness	1.78	3.1745	.037**
Level of dependency on key customers	2.04	4.1801	.021**
Level of collaboration with key customers	1.98	3.9054	.024**
Average length of business relationships with key customers[3]	1.36	1.8456	.087*
Pressure exerted by key customers	1.58	2.4865	.047**
Pressure exerted by technology experts	2.00	3.9983	.023**
Pseudo R^2 [4]		58.37%	
Level of significance		.0000***	

Table 5-4 Determinants of the use of Web-based IOISs to exchange inventory information with key customers

The Tobit regression shows that each of these hypotheses is confirmed. Results also show that the six determinants explain 58.37% of the variance in the use of Web-based IOISs to exchange inventory information with key customers, which confirm the validity of the proposed model.

Our findings indicate that a manufacturing firm's organizational readiness, its business relationships, and the pressure exerted by key customers and technology experts all affect its future use of Web-based IOISs to share inventory information with its key customers. Therefore, these findings may reveal to practitioners the circumstances in which manufacturing firms should adopt Web-based IOISs to share inventory information with their key customers. Indeed, this study emphasizes the need for managers to consider the characteristics of their supply chain relationships, and not just technological factors, before they decide to adopt an interorganizational innovation such as a Web-based IOIS to support their collaborative processes with partners. Demonstrating the importance of technology experts in the assimilation of Web-based IOISs is another practical contribution this study makes, since we hope this finding will encourage firms to call on technology experts while developing in-house competencies in order to avoid becoming dependent on external resources. Informing governments about the "trigger mechanisms" for innovative e-collaboration is an additional practical contribution of this study since these stimuli can guide public institutions in the development of public policies to encourage firms, particularly SMEs, not only to adopt Web-based IOISs but also to ensure that this innovation is smoothly integrated into their organizational processes and individual behaviors.

Conclusion

Our results demonstrated the positive relationship between each of the determinants, namely organizational readiness, level of dependency on key suppliers, level of collaboration with key suppliers, average length of business relationships with key customers, pressure exerted by key customers and pressure exerted by technology experts, and the manufacturing firms' use of Web-based IOISs to exchange inventory information with key customers.

However, there are several limitations to this study. The first two limitations are conceptual and methodological. First, we did not consider the full set of possible determinants of manufacturing firms to use Web-based IOISs to exchange inventory information with their key customers. And, after the pre-test, some items of the survey instrument were eliminated to shorten the questionnaire. These two limitations, nonetheless, allowed us to reach a larger number of firms, and thus to increase the external validity of our findings. The dilemma of choosing between internal validity and external validity is present in every research process.

The third limitation is methodological. The research model was tested with data collected from a sample of firms derived from an up to-date list of manufacturing firms obtained from a business that specializes in Internet-based direct marketing. Evidently, this limits the reach and the generalizability of our results to all Canadian manufacturing firms, let alone manufacturing firms in other countries. Also, the use of an electronic questionnaire biases the study. However, our sample size compares favorably with previous surveys carried out in the field of e-commerce.

The last limitation is conceptual. As is quite common in the diffusion literature, this study makes the assumption that adopting Web-based IOISs to share inventory information with key customers is good for manufacturing firms. However, as we do not measure the costs and risks related to the adoption of Web-based IOISs by manufacturing firms to share inventory information with their key customers, we do not really evaluate the “goodness” of that decision.

Future research avenues are numerous. As a first step, the research model proposed in this study could be extended and further tested. For example, researchers could attempt to measure the influence of various determinants on manufacturing firms’ use of Web-based IOISs to share other types of information (e.g., product and customer information) with their supply chain partners. Investigating the influence of the use of Web-based IOISs to share inventory information with business partners on various outcome variables (e.g., firm performance, supply chain performance, joint decision making) could also be interesting. Finally, researchers could examine whether the determinants of firms’ use of Web-based IOISs to exchange information with their supply chain partners varies from one country to another and from one manufacturing sector to another.

In a second step, more research could be undertaken to further our knowledge of IOISs. For example, field studies could be performed to identify the critical capabilities and associated benefits of the various types of IOISs used to support the sharing of different types of information between collaborative partners. Case studies could also help researchers identify the critical success factors of various types of IOIS initiatives to support interorganizational collaboration.

Appendix A. survey instrument

Use of Web-based IOISs	Not at all						To a great extent
To what extent does your organization use Web-based IOISs to share inventory information with key customers?	1	2	3	4	5	6	7
Organizational readiness	Completely disagree						Completely agree
Your organization has the necessary management support for the implemention and support of Web-based IOISs	1	2	3	4	5	6	7
Your organization has the necessary financial resources to implement and support Web-based IOISs	1	2	3	4	5	6	7
Staff members within your organization are willing to change the way they work to use Web-based IOISs	1	2	3	4	5	6	7
The IT staff within your organization is knowledgable enough to implement and support Web-based IOISs	1	2	3	4	5	6	7
The non-IT staff within your organization is knowledgable enough to use Web-based IOISs	1	2	3	4	5	6	7
Your organization has an adequate IT infrastructure to implement Web-based IOISs	1	2	3	4	5	6	7
There is an adequate level of integration between your existing information systems to benefit from the use of Web-based IOISs	1	2	3	4	5	6	7

Dependency on key customers							
Do you have a limited number of key customers?	Yes ☐ No ☐						
If yes, what percentage of your total purchases do they represent?	________ %						
Average length of business relationships with key customers							
What it the average length of business relationships with you key customers?	________ months						
Level of collaboration with key customers	Not at all						To a great extent
To what extent does your organization engage in collaborative planning with key customers?	1	2	3	4	5	6	7
To what extent does your organization take joint actions with key customers?	1	2	3	4	5	6	7
Pressure exerted by key customers	Not at all						To a great extent
To what extent do your key customers influence your organization's adoption of IOISs	1	2	3	4	5	6	7
Pressure exerted by technology experts	Not at all						To a great extent
To what extent do the following groups influence your organization's adoption of IOISs? Consultants	1	2	3	4	5	6	7
Integrators	1	2	3	4	5	6	7

CHAPTER SIX

KNOWLEDGE MANAGEMENT FORUM: ON-LINE R&D SUPPORT TOOL FOR SME MANUFACTURES IN QUEBEC

CONSTANCE VAN HORNE, DIANE POULIN, JEAN-MARC FRAYRET AND HEDI KAFFEL

Introduction

The challenges of the new global economy are numerous and seemingly unending. For forest product sector industries in particular, companies find themselves playing catch-up to new environmental regulations, new technologies, changing customer expectations and lower margins. Moreover, the Canadian furniture industry is experiencing ferocious competition from low-wage manufacturers from China combined with the fluctuations in the Canadian dollar, to create a near perfect storm of external pressures. The changes that are required to ensure the industry's sustainability are often radical in nature. This is forcing companies to abandon their traditional *façon de faire* and to look for new knowledge and innovative ideas from outside agencies. In fact, they are increasingly looking to universities or centers of expertise to help find solutions to these new challenges with innovative products, processes and business systems.

This chapter presents an exploratory case study of an example of such a research center working with the Quebec furniture industry. The industry has created, along with government, independent and university research centers, a partnership to confront these global challenges. The mission of PARIM (Partenariat de recherche sur l'industrie du meuble/ Research Partnership in the Furniture Industry) is to be the motor of technological progress in the Quebec furniture industry by structuring efforts in R&D,

technology and knowledge transfer and through the formation of partnerships and alliances to support innovation and competence building.

To facilitate the knowledge and technology transfer processes, the PARIM has created an online knowledge management platform to share and develop knowledge among experts (researchers associated with universities and the centers of expertise) and members of the industry. This paper will investigate how the electronic forum is used and viewed by both researchers and member small and medium sized enterprises (SMEs).

The chapter is organized as follows. The second section will introduce the context of the Quebec furniture industry, the PARIM and describe the functionalities of the forum. The third section will provide a literature review of knowledge and technology transfer from academic-industry research groups to industry. A particular focus will be given to using Internet technologies for transfer to SMEs. Following this will be a description of the various research methods employed in the case study. The fourth section will present the results of the case study and discussion. The final section will provide conclusions and avenues for future research.

1. Context

The PARIM (Partenariat de recherche sur l'industrie du meuble/ Research Partnership in the Furniture Industry) regroups Forintek Canada (an independent research group operating in the Canadian forest products industry), the Université Laval (with the participation of two university-industry centers of expertise FOR@C and CIBISA), the CRIQ (Centre de recherche industrielle du Québec/Industrial Research Centre of Quebec), the Université du Québec à Trois Rivières (with the participation of the Chaire industrielle de recherche sur la productivité et l'innovation en réseau dans le secteur du meuble) and the École nationale du meuble et de l'ébénisterie. In addition to this is the participation of the Association des fabricants de meubles du Québec (AMFQ) which represents nearly 200 firms from the Quebec furniture industry.

1.1. Furniture industry in Canada and Quebec

The furniture industry in Canada largely consists of manufacturers of household furniture and office and institutional furniture. In 2002 there were nearly 3,600 firms employing over 100,000 people and shipped CAN$13.3 billion of goods. Of this, CAN$6.9 billion in goods were exported, almost entirely to the United States (96% of shipments in 2003). Almost 50% of firms produce goods, at least partly, for export markets (Industry Canada). This large focus on exportation and the American market leaves the industry vulnerable to fluctuations in the Canadian-American exchange rate. The fluctuations in the Canadian dollar have had serious impacts on the industry's competitiveness and ability to plan for the future. Additionally, increased competition from China has had a large impact on Canadian firms.

The Province of Quebec is a major player in the Canadian industry. The province's manufacturers produce approximately 30% of total industry shipments, 38% of firms, and 33% of employment. Firms in the Quebec furniture industry are mainly small and medium in size and family-owned, although seven of the ten largest Canadian furniture firms are located in Quebec. After the Canadian-American free trade agreement was signed in 1993, the Quebec industry began to target the American market through specialization and quality improvement (US Commercial Service).

With increasing competition from China, Quebec companies are looking to new strategies and manufacturing processes to compete and differentiate their products. According to the US Commercial Service (2006), Quebec firms are looking to new technologies, lean-manufacturing, just-in-time deliveries, new marketing techniques and customizing services (including mass-customization). These firm-level changes are a reflection of the entire restructuring of the Canadian and Quebec furniture industry. Intra and inter-province competition has been replaced by a more united vision of the industry's future. The PARIM is an example of this phenomenon and is explained in further detail in the next sub-section.

1.2 PARIM (Partenariat de recherche sur l'industrie du meuble/ Research partnership in the Furniture Industry)

The mission of PARIM is to be the motor of technological progress in the Quebec furniture industry by structuring efforts in R&D, technology and knowledge transfer and through the formation of partnerships and alliances to support innovation and competence building. This mission was chosen as it is widely accepted that unique competencies and innovation are the only sustainable sources of competitive advantage for a firm. The objectives of PARIM are to:

1. Respond to the short-term R&D needs of the industry by creating synergy between researchers and industry practitioners;
2. Create a world-class R&D network;
3. Accelerate the innovation cycle;
4. Accelerate the commercialization/implantation of new products/processes;
5. Create a synergy among the member experts of the PARIM to avoid "reinventing the wheel".

These five objectives are all to realize the goals of increasing the competitiveness of the Quebec furniture industry and to ensure its long-term survival. To facilitate the knowledge and technology transfer processes the PARIM has developed a knowledge management platform to share and develop knowledge among experts (researchers associated with the centers of expertise) and members of the industry.

1.3 Knowledge management forum

The forum is moderated by an employee of one of the member research organizations. There are two categories of members of the PARIM. There are individual SMEs (represented by one or more employees) and experts from the participating research groups. Participants each have an individual log-in name and password, and access to the forum and associated virtual library are restricted to members.

The forum is divided into different categories, representing different subjects that are of interest to members (i.e. new business models, new process technologies, machines, etc.). Questions are posted to the appropriate section, or are sent by members of the PARIM, either directly to the forum or through the moderator (in case the participant wishes to remain anonymous). The question is then available to view by everyone and the moderator also sends the question to the expert (or experts) that he deems best able to respond to the question. Experts are requested to respond to the question within 48 hours, and if they are not able to respond they are asked to inform the moderator as soon as possible. However, questions are also answered by other members, and "conversations" can develop amongst members for any question or response. Every time there is a question or answer posted to the forum an email notifying all registered participants of the fact.

The experts associated with the PARIM are all members of individual research groups, which are member organizations of the larger group. While the PARIM is an amalgamation of research groups and industry members, it also operates as a separate group that shares many characteristics with university-industry research centers. These characteristics include organizing both applied and basic research projects, participation funding, and resources from universities, industry and government groups, and outputs that are both scientific in nature (i.e. academic articles) and applied (i.e. question to the forum) in nature. In particular, there is a strong emphasis on knowledge and technology transfer from researchers to industry (Van Horne et al. 2007). The next section presents a review of the literature concerning these groups and the transfer processes they employ. A particular focus will be given to transfer processes using internet technologies.

2. Literature review

2.1. Academic-industry research centers

As all industries become increasingly knowledge based, and as products, processes and business systems become more complex, companies are turning to academic research groups to assist them in their innovation processes (Van Horne et al. 2005). At the same time universities and researchers have moved beyond their traditional roles of teaching and research to become "entrepreneurs" (Etzkowitz 2003) of their knowledge, skills and research results. Government has also played a role in encouraging this new academic role.

As a result, new relationships have developed in the form of academic-industry partnerships and research centers. These collaborations provide both technologies (new products, processes, business models, etc.) and services (in the form of knowledge training, consulting, recruitment of highly qualified personnel, interns, etc.) to firms (D'Este and Patel 2007; Etzkowitz and Leydesdorff 2000). In addition, services are provided to governments through economic development (Etzkowitz 2003) and to universities and researchers through additional funding, access to industry research problems and data, increased reputation, etc. (D'Este and Patel 2007).

Often these centers are formed to address a need in an important industry in a country or region. These centers are focused in their research and operate within a specific context; however, they do much more than basic research. Extension activities play a vital part of their role in industry. The transfer of technologies and innovative knowledge and assisting in the implementation of innovations to create effective value is an important part of their work. There is much debate and questioning by researchers and transfer professionals as to what are the best tools and methods to use to transfer abstract concepts such as supply chain management from researchers to industry practitioners.

The mission of these centers may serve various purposes and "customers/audiences" according to the sources of its funding, but a common goal can be extrapolated: to create value using research and innovation. A center works in collaborative networks with researchers from other centers and universities, government agencies and practitioners from the industry to advance science and stimulate continuous knowledge development and innovation in the industry. However, the tools and methods used to develop and implement this new knowledge and innovation have changed over the years as companies have changed their focus from innovations in products to innovations in processes (Just in Time, Total Quality Management) and most recently to innovations in business systems (Enterprise Resource Planning, Advanced Planning and Scheduling Systems) (Van Horne et al. 2005).

2.2. Knowledge management and transfer

Technology transfer involves the transfer of an object or tool that is the explicit embodiment of knowledge which is capable of changing the environment. Knowledge transfer involves learning (either on an individual or organizational level) techniques or ways of thinking, theories, principals (Gopalakrishnan and Santoro 2004), or the "why" and "how" of a technology. Theoretically the differences are obvious, however there are several similarities.

Both of these concepts – technology transfer and knowledge transfer - are regarded as vital to the value-creating activities of a firm. Even more, they have been seen as a strategic good, critical to a competitive domestic economy (Kremic 2003). They are also both seen as important value-creating activities that occur over time and within a collaborative context. Gopalakrishnan and Santoro (2004) suggest that there are seven issues common to both: strategy, structure, shared values, support systems, styles, skills and staff. The authors are clear in the differences in each issue between the two concepts. For example, technology transfer is usually a bottom-up process as it involves implementing a tool that has to be put to use by the operators of that tool. Therefore, employees need to have the skills necessary to effectively exploit the tool and they also need to "support" the technology in question or the implementation will not be a success. Conversely, transferring a business plan would require a top-down process as management needs to support and understand the concepts (know-why and know-how) before it can be applied. Both technology and knowledge transfer take place with person to person contact and interaction and these contacts are often maintained and supported with information and communication technologies (ICT).

2.3. Using ICT for knowledge transfer

The technologies that are used for knowledge management include network knowledge infrastructure, knowledge sharing intranets, extranets and external knowledge sharing and groupware technologies and collaboration (Seng et al. 2002). Transfer occurs at many different levels: from individual to individual, from individual to group, from stored knowledge to individual, from group to individual, etc. Knowledge transfer is supported by open communication flows and often through ICT tools. Alavi and Leidner (2001) write that there are five main elements of knowledge transfer:

1. Value perception of the knowledge;
2. Willingness to share knowledge;
3. Existence and support of transmission channels (formal and informal);
4. Willingness to accept knowledge;
5. Capacity to understand received knowledge (absorptive capacity).

Once knowledge is transferred there is often a presumption of absorption and application. Applying knowledge is of course the key the process that supports competitive advantage. There are three common methods or mechanisms that are used to integrate or apply knowledge in an organization (Alavi and Leidner 2001):

- Directives which includes rules, standards, procedures and instructions;
- Organizational routines which include process specifications, protocols and coordinated patterns;

- Self-contained task teams charged with integrating knowledge into an organization's product, process or business system.

The benefits associated with using ICT for transfer processes are particularly evident in SMEs. They provide easy and rapid access to external sources of knowledge and erase some of the constraints associated with the innovative capacity of SMEs, such as the lack of dedicated R&D departments, or the lack of necessary resources to search and apply new knowledge (Corso et al. 2003; Thomas et al. 2004). The next section outlines the particularities of knowledge transfer to SME and the use of ICT in these processes.

2.4. Knowledge transfer to SME

Thomas et al. (2004) studied SME manufacturers in Wales and found that there is a strong and increasingly important link between small business and universities. It is important not only for current projects, but also for the continuing growth of technology and innovation. The authors also point out that universities can provide a small business with resources and facilities that it may not have access to due to its limited financial position, and that universities receive experience for students and facilities and the opportunity to form a working relationship with the company (which can lead to further collaboration). In fact, one study found that that the universities that provided the education and training services benefited from the scheme, rather than the participating SME (Macdonald et al. 2007).

This highlights some of the difficulties associated with transfer processes to SMEs. Macdonald et al. (2007) found that managers of SMEs were generally less convinced that education and training led to innovation than the providers of the education and training were, and therefore more reluctant to participate (although often participation was provided free of charge). Other difficulties have been noted:

- Knowledge tends to be tacit/informal/not recorded;
- Know-how in SMEs may not be valued as highly as it might be;
- Lack of know-how may be hard to talk about in SMEs;
- Short-term approaches to knowledge gaps may work sufficiently to make change appear unnecessary;
- Know-how in an SMEs may easily be lost or fragmented when the owner sells the business or retires (CEN Workshop 2004).

Although ICT can be used to reduce the physical distance between researchers and practitioners, their psychological distance is harder to bridge and depends largely on the interest of the practitioner in the research being done (St-Pierre et al. 2007). Furthermore, the authors suggest that for these collaborations to be successful there need to be bridges between the two worlds, and the creation of mutual spaces that favor exchanges and also the development of scientific and practical knowledge.

There is a fine line, especially with SMEs, between consultancy and transfer. It is important that researchers' interaction with practitioners creates scientific knowledge through an iterative process of interaction with practitioners. Otherwise, a linear transaction would suggest that the researcher is acting as a "free" consultant. Conversely, the knowledge and technology created needs to be of "value" to the practitioner or there is no benefit to participation.

St-Pierre et al. (2007) suggest there are several factors that can lead to success in these transfer processes:

- Mutual respect of the expertise and knowledge of each actor and the desire for each actor to benefit from the project;
- Capacity to use a common language so that each actor understands the other;
- Motivation and interest on the part of the actors for the project;
- Obtaining funding from granting organizations so that researchers are not dependent on practitioners;
- Multi-disciplinary team, involvement of graduate students and the possibilities of publications at different phases of the development of the project.

An exploratory case study was used to investigate the particularities of knowledge transfer from university-industry research groups to SMEs through the use of ICT and how it is used and viewed by both researchers and practitioners.

3. Methodology

Case studies are appropriate when current perspectives in a domain appear to be inadequate in accurately describing and explaining phenomena. Yin (2003) explains that there are five different applications of case study research: explanation, description, illustration, exploration and meta-evaluation. The purpose of this case study was to explore the phenomenon.

There are six sources of evidence that can be used for case studies (Yin 2003); all (excepting the last) were used in this case study:

- Documents
    - Used to corroborate and augment evidence from other sources;
- Archival records
    - retrieval of data;
- Interviews
    - Essential source of case study information;
    - Open-ended, focused or formal survey;
- Direct observation
    - See the actually workings of the phenomena studied;
- Participant-observation
    - Ability to perceive reality from the viewpoint of someone "inside" the case study;
- Physical artefacts

A single case study was used and chosen because it is an excellent example of the phenomenon and there were opportunities for unusual research access available to the authors (Eisenhardt and Graebner 2007).

3.1. Participant and direct observation

Direct and participant observation was used throughout the research process. The authors have posed questions on the forum, responded to questions as "experts" and passively read the questions and answers on the forum. In addition, several face-to-face meetings and two conferences were attended to acquire an improved understanding of the industry and the particular context of the phenomenon.

3.2. Surveys and questionnaires

A brief survey was sent to the designated contact person in each member company of the PARIM in May 2006 regarding their knowledge and use of the forum. The forum had been online from November of 2005 and as it was a "new" transfer tool feedback was seen as a valuable source of information to improve the use and value of the knowledge platform and forum. In total 66 companies were contacted through email and telephone calls and 34 responses were gathered. Of those, eight had heard of the forum but had not visited and the others had at least logged on once. (These data were varied using forum archives).

A questionnaire was sent to the 85 experts listed in the PARIM database. A total of 11 responses were gathered. Of these, one expert had never heard of the forum. Of the ten remaining nine had used the forum at least once (seven had answered a question and two had asked a question).

3.3. Interviews

Two interviews were conducted with two employees of a hardwood furniture SME (100 employees) that manufactures for the American export market. Because 90% of their goods are exported to the United States, they have been affected by the rise in the value of the Canadian dollar. However, the reason given by both employees for a loss of 200 jobs since 2005 was the rise in the competition from Chinese furniture manufacturers. The company has several on-going projects with government research and university-industry research groups. One of them had answered a question, but both accessed the forum when interesting questions were asked, or to see the answers provided. Both admitted that they used the forum as another method of technological intelligence and to find out what problems other companies face, because they might face the same ones in the future and would know where to find the necessary information to solve the problem.

4. Results and discussion

A content analysis of the forum archives indicates that participation rates have increased since its inception (see Table 6-1). Access by industrial members appears to have increased substantially, especially compared to the number of accesses by experts. All companies surveyed had access to Internet and email, as did all experts. A summary of the results of the survey, questionnaire and interview is provided in Table 6-2.

	Winter 1/2006	Spring 2/2006	Summer 3/2006	Fall 4/2006	Winter 1/2007	Spring 2/2007
Number of accesses	6973	8342	9724	12549	11542	11064
Number of industrials who accessed	1467	2137	3889	5243	4642	4460
Number of experts who accessed	5506	6205	5835	7306	6900	6604
Number of questions on the forum	19	14	20	33	16	20
Number of answers	60	34	62	83	29	62
Average number of answers	3.2	2.4	3.1	2.5	1.8	3.1
Average response time	8h42min	8h42min	8h43min	9h12min	10h22min	10h25min

Table 6-1 Statistics from the forum

Comparing the companies that indicated that they had used the forum in the survey and a list of companies that had received a personalized training session with a member from the AMFQ concerning how to use the forum and the knowledge management platform, indicates a strong correlation between the two. Members who had not had the training were much less inclined (or able) to use this tool.

An interesting finding is that companies use the forum to contact both experts and other companie,s and that they are willing to respond to the questions of others with their own personal experiences. A recent example of such an exchange is taken directly from the website. The question was asked by a member of a research group and answered by a practitioner in an SME (the question and answer have been translated):

(Asked at 15:38)

Does anyone know if specific guidelines have been established to evaluate the performance of sanding bands? There are so many choices on the market. Unfortunately few companies are able to objectively measure and evaluate performance.

(Answered at 16:34)

Hello,

It all depends on what criteria you use to study your belts. If the quality of the sanding is the same, then you can always compare the number of linear feet or the average number of square feet sanded with one belt versus its price. This will allow you to refer to a cost per square foot, which could then become your reference for future tests. If you do tests on a production line, it is enough to check the quality of the sanding when you do continuous finishing. However, if you don't do finishing, then you can still do a paint test at regular intervals.

This method is less "scientific", except that it does give a basis for comparison. Let me know if you have other testing methods.

	Reasons given for participating	Reasons given for not participating	Benefits perceived/ received	Problems encountered	Ways to improve
Experts	- required to - received email from moderator - wanted to ask a question - interested in questions/ answers - curious	- no questions relevant to domain of expertise email received from forum put into spam (too many email received) - lack of time	- many interesting questions - pertinent questions and answers to industry problems - supports regular research activities - allow to better transfer research results and knowledge - increase network of contacts in the industry	- too many email received - domain of expertise is not respected and all questions and answers are sent to all experts	- only send notification of questions and answers posted to the forum once a week (summarized) - increase number of face-to-face meetings to encourage more ties between experts and companies
Members of SME	- technological intelligence - with increased Chinese competition realize need to work with other Quebec companies - good tool to communicate with other companies of the industry - want to learn from experts and experience of other companies	- no time - no interest - not used to using the forum - not familiar enough with the PARIM or the forum - prefer face-to-face contact - no R&D priority (need to survive) - do not need outside assistance	- creates links between firms (can respond to one another's questions) - can be used to communicate to industry - interesting information - useful information - rapid response to questions not able to answer with internal resources - information useful for reflection - introduction to new concepts	- problems with username and password - employee with username and password left the company - difficulty finding information - too many email received	- try to post more timely information - more benchmarking reports should be posted

Table 6-2 Case study results

A review of all the questions and answers on the forum indicates that this is a typical example of an exchange. The practitioners at times replace the "experts" and the forum is used as a platform for increased communication and mutual support amongst the SMEs and practitioners. In fact, those who used and use the forum indicate that there are real connections being made between researchers and practitioners and between SMEs themselves.

Another interesting finding is that there is value created for both the individual SMEs who ask the questions and the researchers (experts) who are charged with answering the queries on the forum, according to the gathered data. However, the definition of value was not expressed in tangible terms and would be difficult to quantify with tradition metrics of value. For example, the creation of links and connects between the different actors of the Quebec forest products industry was a common benefit of both practitioners and experts. Yet, with current metrics this created value is difficult to measure, due to its intangible nature.

While there are benefits and value created, these benefits incur costs. Results indicate that the creation and continuation of such a forum requires support for training participants in its use, through the organization of face-to-face meetings and through the continuous improvement of its functionalities through feed-back from all members of the research group (both participants and non-participants of the forum).

Conclusion

The challenges of the new global economy are numerous and many SMEs simply do not have the necessary internal R&D capabilities to develop adequate responses to these challenges. To overcome these weaknesses, SMEs can look to universities or centers of expertise to help find solutions to these new challenges with innovative products, processes and business systems.

The online knowledge management forum developed to create links between researchers and companies and to stop "reinventing the wheel" appears to be making some headway towards those goals. There also appears to be mutual support amongst practitioners, made possible with the virtual meeting space, which is of real value for creating a stronger regional or provincial industry going into the future.

The general research question of this work was to investigate how the forum was used by researchers and practitioners. In fact, the forum is used for several purposes, including networking, technical intelligence and a desire to share personal knowledge and experience to help other members of the industry (both researchers and practitioners).

Other observations from the study of the PARIM and the use of its forum indicate that while participation rates remain relatively stable (with a slight decrease) there are real connections being made between researchers and practitioners and even between SMEs themselves. In addition, there is value created for both the individual SMEs whom ask the questions and the researchers (experts) who are charged with answering the queries on the forum. However, « Results indicate that creating and maintaining this kind of forum will involve investments of time and money in terms of training, organizational meetings and solicitation and evaluation of feedback.

Although there has been value created, it is difficult to measure or quantify. More research will need to be done to develop metrics that can be used to quantity this value. This would assist policy makers and companies better evaluate new tools such as these.

Another interesting aspect to investigate would be the effect that the PARIM and the forum have on the creation of a network, considered so valuable for industry prosperity by many authors (Pittaway et al. 2004; Powell et al. 1996).

CHAPTER SEVEN

ANTECEDENTS OF ERP ASSIMILATION: THE CASES OF A MEDIUM-SIZED AND A LARGE MANUFACTURING COMPANY

RAFA KOUKI, ROBERT PELLERIN AND DIANE POULIN

Introduction

Since their emergence, enterprise resource planning (ERP) systems have been promoted as a critical technology in an increasingly complex and knowledge- intensive economy. Due to their increased capabilities and continuous evolution, ERP systems have moved out of manufacturing workshops and large companies into not only various industries but also to small and medium sized companies (Loh and Koh 2004).

In spite of the large-scale adoption of enterprise systems and the concomitant momentum that these systems are gaining worldwide, attaining their expected benefits is still a challenging task. It has been argued that if planned, implemented and assimilated properly, ERP systems can significantly improve information flow, streamline internal processes and hence develop the firm's efficiency and its competitive advantage (Beard and Sumner 2004; Muscatello and Parente 2006). By using a common operating platform and enhancing network capabilities, different departments - and even different sites - of the company can communicate instantly between each other and can access and transfer information more easily, something that would enable a better control over operations (Dowlatshahi 2005).

Other advantages of ERP systems include the integration and the synchronization of the firm's supply chain activities (which means a better and faster customer service), reduced cycle time and increased productivity, increased flexibility by enabling easier access to the firm's data, a reduction in redundant entry and reduction in process time, the economization of resources by quickly identifying problematic areas, and an increased autonomy in data use and access which supports and facilitates the decision making process in the different firm's departments and sites (Amoako-Gyampah and Salam 2004; Dowlatshahi 2005).

Despite these advantages, several ERP implementations have not lived up their adopters' expectations, and horror stories and failure experiences litter the ERP landscape. Several reasons for ERP project failures have been cited in the literature (Botta–Genoulaz et al. 2005). Most of the reasons referred to in the literature, however, deal with the early stages of the project (i.e., the selection, the preparation and the implementation stages). These include the wrong choice of software, the inappropriate timing of the project, improper planning, business process reengineering and implementation, lack of resources (material and human resources), improper employee involvement, lack of good communication and inconsistent management support (Barker and Frolick 2003; Umble et al. 2003).

The post-implementation stage and its issues have not been sufficiently addressed in the literature (Botta-Genoulaz et al. 2005; Nicolau and Bhattacharya 2006), in spite of its importance,. Problems could also emerge after the implementation process and could result in several problems including total failure. It was argued that ERP failure could occur when the installed system is underutilized and, hence, many of the idiosyncratic features were fully extended by their target users (Davenport 1998; Jasperson et al. 2005; Shehab et al. 2004). Underutilization and rejection of the system are but two symptoms of more serious problems that have to be addressed during the post-implementation stage (Botta-Genoulaz et al. 2005).

Although there has been a growing interest in the post-implementation stage, there is still a need to investigate the different issues and aspects of this phase in the ERP project life cycle. Given the potential benefits that an ERP system can generate for a company on the one hand and the large financial commitment that it requires on the other, it is important to understand and to investigate the determinants that facilitate the assimilation process of ERP systems in a company. Moreover, given the increasing adoption of ERP systems by small and medium sized enterprises (SMEs) and their need to address the problems that could arise once the system is implemented, it is essential for these companies to understand the determinants that facilitate ERP assimilation. The objective of the chapter is to present the experience of two manufacturing firms - a large company and an SME that have adopted an ERP system - and to investigate the different factors that facilitate or hamper ERP adoption.

The remainder of the chapter is organized as follows. First, the research methodology is explained. Next, the case analysis is exposed. The results are then presented and discussed. Finally, the chapter concludes with the main lessons learned from this analysis.

1. The ERP assimilation concept

Organizational information technology (IT) assimilation has been of an increasing interest to researchers in information systems for more than a decade (Chatterjee et al. 2002; Cooper and Zmud 1990; Fichman and Kemerer 1997). IT assimilation is considered to be a central objective and an essential outcome of the adoption and implementation efforts (Armstrong and Sambamurthy 1999). It has been argued in previous research that prior to being able to come up with a successful business, a new technology needs to be fully integrated and embedded into the value chain of the given firm (Delone and Mclean 2002).

Assimilation definitions in information systems (IS) vary among researchers. Fichman and Kemerer (1997) and Fichman (2000) consider assimilation to be the process which extends from the initial awareness of the innovation to its potential acquisition and wide-scale deployment. Hence assimilation includes awareness, interest, evaluation, trial, commitment, and deployment (more limited than general deployment). Assimilation has also been defined as the extent to which the technology is used in a comprehensive and integrated way and becomes embedded in the firm's work processes and value chain activities (Armstrong and Sambamurthy 1999; Chatterjee et al. 2002; Markus et al. 2000; Purvis et al. 2001). For Bajwa et al. (2004) all the ERP life cycle stages represent the ERP assimilation process. It includes awareness for the need of implementing ERP, package selection, preparation, implementation and operation. So assimilation refers to the extent to which the organization has progressed from understanding the ERP systems' potential and functionalities to mastering and deploying them in their key value chain processes and various managerial activities and decision levels. When compared to Cooper Zmud's stage model (1990) (Figure 7-1), assimilation represents the three post-implementation stages of acceptance, routinization and infusion.

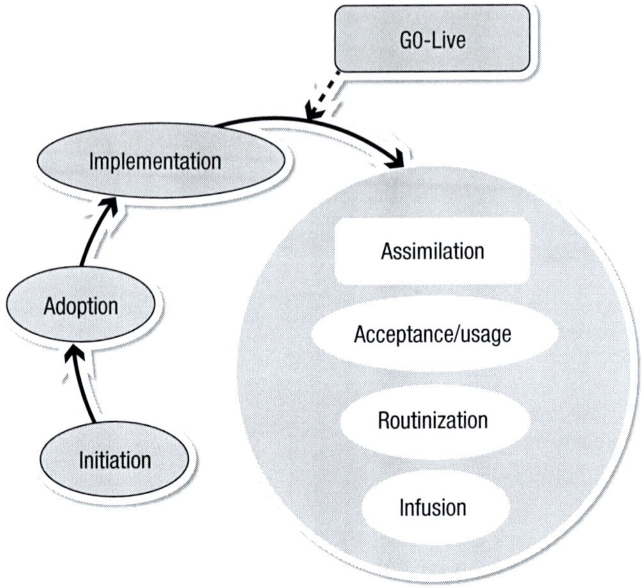

Figure 7-1 ERP assimilation process in relation to the other processes

1.1. Conceptual framework

Tornatzky and Fleischer (1990) suggested that the external environment, the organizational context, and the technological context were related to the failure or success of IS applications. ERP literature (Markus et al. 2000; Musaji 2005; Umble et al. 2003) has also emphasized the importance of contingency factors in ERP implementation and benefit realization. Based on this previous research, the focus is put on a set of technological, organizational and environmental factors that may impact ERP assimilation, as presented in Figure 7-2. These are: ERP attributes and IT expertise of the technological context, top management support, absorptive capacity, strategic alignment, user involvement and reward system for the organizational context and vendor support, consultant effectiveness and the institutional pressures for the environmental context.

Table 7-1 provides a description of the factors of the conceptual framework.

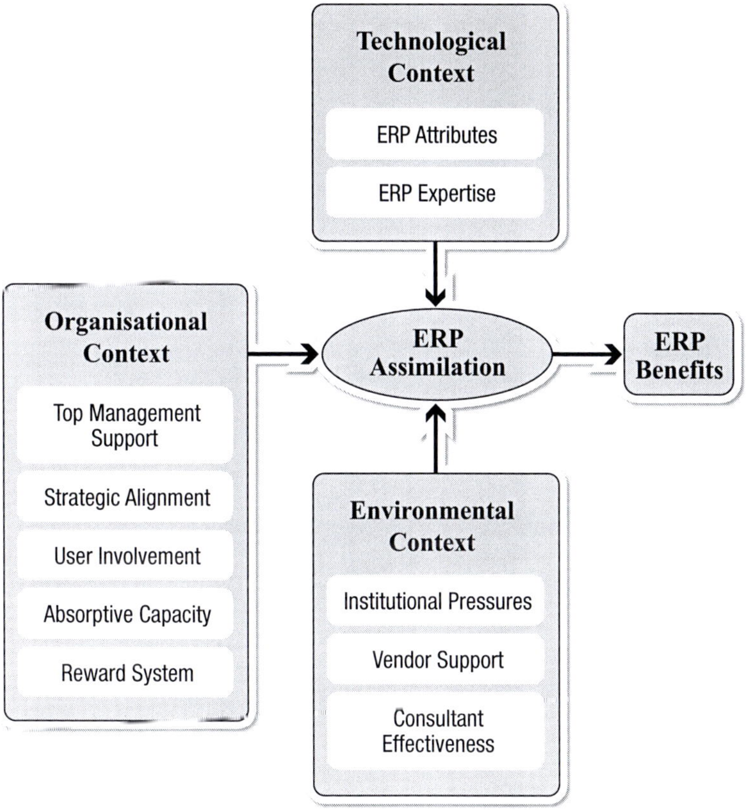

Figure 7-2 ERP Assimilation conceptual framework

Variable	Description
ERP attributes	Describes possible ERP systems' technical attributes that might influence the acceptance and the assimilation rate of the system by its users
IT expertise	Describes the IT people's competence in maintaining, updating and supporting the ERP users
Top management championship	Refers to the extent that top management supports, directly and indirectly, and commits to the continuous use, upgrade and progress of the ERP
Absorptive capacity	Refers to the firm's efforts to encourage learning in the organization, including the organization's commitment to learning principally by training and putting in place procedures to capture, codify and disseminate ERP knowledge
Strategic alignment	Describes the continuous fit between the ERP system (which is part of the IT infrastructure), the business strategy, the IT strategy and the organizational structure
User involvement	Refers to the psychological engagement of users with the ERP system by considering their problem and suggestions about the system
Reward system	Refers to the changes that the reward system in the company might have undergone after the introduction of the ERP system
Institutional pressures	Refers to the mimetic, coercive and normative pressures that a company might undergo to encourage further assimilation of the system
Vendor/Consultant support	Describes the level and the effectiveness of vendors and external consultants during the system's upgrades

Table 7-1 Description of the framework variables

2. Research methodology

When behavioral events cannot be adequately controlled, and when little is known about a phenomenon due to the lack of theory, a qualitative approach such as the case study method is highly recommended as an alternative means to gather evidence and to understand complex phenomena (Eisenhardt 1989; Stuart et al. 2002; Yin 1994). Yin (1994) defined a case study as an "empirical inquiry that: (a) investigates a contemporary phenomenon within real life context, especially when (b) the boundaries between phenomenon and context are not clearly evident". ERP systems projects represent a major undertaking in a firm, often involving all company departments and processes, requiring significant investments of both time and money that could extend over periods ranging from months to years. All of these factors contribute to the ERP systems' initiative complexity. Consequently, a quantitative methodology would not allow for an in-depth understanding of the firm's and the interviewees' experiences with the system.

The analysis of ERP assimilation at the post-implementation stage is based on two Canadian manufacturing companies. The criterion used to select the case study companies was that each of the case studies should have implemented ERP software to its operations. For reasons of confidentiality, we have given assumed names to each company: Food Co. for the SME and Plastic Co. for the large company.

Interviews and observations were the primary sources of data and archival online and paper documentation were the secondary sources. The interviews were conducted within the span of 5 months. Four to five members were interviewed in each company with each interview varying between 50 to 80 minutes. Respondents include: the vice president (VP) operations/production, the VP marketing, the VP finance, the VP Information technology, and a plant manager. Some key respondents were visited and/or contacted more than once to validate the collected information. Guidelines about data validation and data accuracy were followed during and after the realization of the interviews. A questionnaire in the form of semi structured questions was developed using the 10 constructs presented in Table 7-1. These questions were used to guide the interview sessions. All interviews were recorded with the approval of the respondents. The interviews were then transcribed and in case of doubt and lack of clarity, the data were rechecked with the informants. That data was then reduced into codes and into categories that correspond to the set of the new and originally identified themes.

3. Case analysis

3.1 Company profiles

In this section the background of the two chosen companies and their need to implement the ERP system are presented. The profiles of both organizations are summarized in Table 7-2.

Food Co.

Food Co. is a leading medium sized food processing company with annual sales of about $200 million CAN and 500 employees across 5 production facilities. Its SAP R/3 ERP system was implemented in 1998 using a Big-Bang approach. Tax changes, the year 2000 problem and the increasing requirements of their clients' needs strongly encouraged Food Co. to adopt an ERP system. The company used to have several "*information silos*". Even though the IT department tried to group the company's data in a single data warehouse, it was not possible to coordinate the different sets of "*information silos*" to have a unique view of the firm. At the time when the system was implemented, all basic modules such as finance, managerial finance, asset management, sales, purchases, warehouse management, time management, pay, human resource management, and maintenance were implemented. The system at Food Co. was deployed in all the company's departments. The respondents assert that the system perfectly satisfied the business needs in terms of integrity and integration. The system is mostly used for operational and managerial control. Even though it has been implemented for about 10 years, the ERP at Food Co. is not directly used to make strategic decisions. Likewise, planning decisions are made outside the ERP system, as the operations manager considers it to be too complicated compared to the other software that they use. It is important to stress, however, that the basic source of data for both strategic and planning decisions is the ERP system.

Plastic Co.

Plastic Co. is one of the leading North American producers of plastic products. The company employs more than 1000 people operating in 4 facilities in the provinces of Quebec and New Brunswick and a network of sales offices and warehouses in Canada and the United States. The company manufactures over 400 products which are marketed to several industries including food, chemical, forest products, petrochemical, construction and integrated waste management industries. Prior to the implementation of the ERP system, Plastic Co. had three separate systems; one of them was the main manufacturing system. As Plastic Co. needed to upgrade their system, the latter's vendor advised the company that the system would not be supported anymore. Plastic Co. decided then to go with a single integrated system. Note that the ERP project was part of a bigger project of continuous improvement in the company. The process started in February 2004 with choosing the system. In December 2004, the company switched to the ERP system, in the two Quebec plants, following a Big Bang approach. One year later the system was implemented in the New Brunswick plant. The third plant in Quebec was planned to receive the ERP system two months later but the project was postponed until September 2007.

The system at Plastic Co. was at a stabilization stage. The ERP team is still struggling with several problems such as redundancy, the use of parallel systems, the lack of understanding by users and even some managers of the system's value and potential, and the implementation of new modules. When it comes to operations management, the VP of operations, who already has experience with ERP systems, is a strong advocate of the system. He argues that JD Edwards is satisfying several needs of managerial control decisions in the three plants where the system was implemented. At the time when interviews were made, we were informed that extra reports were being built in order to provide a wider and multifaceted view of the firm's operations. A maintenance module was also planned to be implemented during the following months. Similar to Food Co., planning is done with separate software as "*JDE lacks the flexibility that real planning software has*". Nevertheless, the data used for planning was imported from JDE. In terms of integration, the system was not yet implemented in all the company's business processes and plants. Even though "*many information flow barriers*" have fallen between several business processes there was still work to be done in order to fully integrate the firm's business processes. It is worth noting that, according to the VP of IT, the arrival of the new CEO and new VPs who had a better understanding of the system's potential, accelerated and facilitated the system's assimilation efforts. Table 7-2 provides a summarized description of the two companies.

	Food Co	Plastic Co
Industry sector	Cookie and cracker manufacturing	Molded plastic products for several industries (food, chemical, forest products, petrochemical, construction, etc.)
Number of employees	About 500	About 1000
Sales (as of December 31st, 2006, in millions of Canadian dollars)	More than $200	More than $200
Type of system used	SAP	JD Edwards
Implementation date	October 1997	December 2004
Reason for system selection	• Suitable for the firm's operations • "Felt" that SAP was the best solution for them	• Requires less people to support the system than other products • Less complex than other systems • Satisfies business needs (mainly financial)
Drivers for adopting ERP system	• Y2K problem • Clients' pressure to have timely and integrated information • Need to have a system that evolves with increasing sales and firm requirements • Need to provide detailed information for taxation purposes • Need to integrate the firm's functions and processes	• Integration of the 4 companies' financial data with the hope that the others would follow • Previous manufacturing information system was outdated • Need to integrate the firm's functionalities
Post-implementation issues	• Sales manager still hostile to the system (importance of age and seniority) • Evening and night shifts lack appropriate support	• Lack of system understanding • Users lack IT and ERP proficiency: heavy dependence on ERP/IT team due to inadequate user training • Heavy workload for the IT department: lack of programming

	Food Co	Plastic Co
		• Use of parallel systems in several departments of the company • ERP/IT expertise turnover • Employee turnover (extra training costs of new employees) • Users perceived their traditional methods of work as being easier and more efficient than using the ERP • Problems with data quality and integrity • Culture of financial support for product innovation and development vs. IT and business process innovations • Effect of seniority, IT proficiency, and position on user involvement
Current situation of the company	• The company enjoys a leading position in its industry ERP perceived as vital for the company and as the capital tool that helped realizing that success • 90% of the system capacity is exploited • Long term planning realized using another system • Continue to expand its system with new modules and to deploy extra functionalities of the existing modules • ERP used for operational and tactical decisions (data control and process control)	• The company has a competitive position in the industry. It was planning to implement the ERP in the third plant and to implement the maintenance module. • Finance module is the best deployed module while operations are still experiencing problems due to the lack of users commitment and involvement with the system • Just about 30 to 40% of the system capacities were used • ERP represent the information backbone of the firm but it just serves the transactional needs of the company

Table 7-2 Food Co. and Plastic Co. Profiles

3.2 Case study analyses

This section describes each of the constructs and presents a summary of the findings of the two case studies for each variable. Respondents' statements were quoted when appropriate.

3.2.1 ERP attributes

It has been argued that ERP attributes affect user satisfaction and hence the technology's assimilation and diffusion (Moore and Benbasat 1991; Wu and Wang 2006). Wu and Wang (2006) suggest that eleven ERP system characteristics are basic in assessing user satisfaction. These are: ERP system information accuracy, timeliness, reliability, response time and completeness, output requirement (the layout design and flexibility of the output content), relevancy (the degree of congruence between user tasks and ERP functions), system stability, auditing and control (type of auditing rendered by the system), ease of use and usefulness of the system for the user. Flexibility was considered in the literature to be another key characteristic of ERP systems and an essential requirement for the companies (Gupta and Kohli 2006). Indeed, the ERP system's flexibility would allow it to support various business lines and it would enable the addition of modules (software segments) to support supplementary functions and business processes (Ahituv et al. 2002; Shehab et al. 2004).

In the case of Food Co., the ERP system's modularity and flexibility enabled some users, mainly superusers, to stretch the system horizontally by adding small programs which satisfy the users' needs without changing the system's core. Unlike the case of Food Co., system complexity and issues with data accuracy, reliability and timeliness in Plastic Co. resulted in several issues such as redundancy, low system deployment and a lack of satisfaction with the system outputs. The VP of operations asserted that *"there (was) a continuous comparison between JDE's reports and Excel's reports. In case of divergence, Excel's reports (were) given priority over JDE's"*. These problems were mainly due to a lack of training, a lack of appropriate communication and the hasty go-live.

3.2.2 IT expertise

IT expertise refers to the ability to support users and managers in properly deploying the system by providing the required maintenance, refinement and adjustments of the system. Many of the challenging issues of ERP systems emerge once the system installation is complete and the ERP team is disbanded (Musaji 2005). This requires a competent internal IT team that can provide the necessary support for users as well as appropriate system maintenance.

Food Co.'s IT team was described as being "*excellent, very competent and skilled*". They are directly involved with the users by providing them with the required help and assistance. Moreover the operations manager, who participated in the ERP project and who was a superuser, was highly involved with the system users, providing assistance and guidance, developing small programs to make the most of the system's capabilities in his department.

At Plastic Co., the IT department was responsible for the IT systems in the 4 plants. Given the size of the company, one respondent argued that the workload of the IT team is too heavy given the system and the users' requirements. The fact that the system is not stable yet and that users are not yet acquainted with the type of reports that the system produces leads to lots of troubleshooting, customization and system maintenance requirements. In spite of these difficulties, the IT people at Plastic Co. are considered to be very efficient and competent and an important facilitator of the assimilation process of the system in the company.

3.2.3 Top management championship

Top management championship refers to the extent that top management supports and commits to the continuous use of the ERP. It has long been argued that this factor is the most predictive determinant of ERP project success (Somers and Nelson 2004). Given the continuous technological developments of ERP systems and their endless requirements, top management support should be sustained as long as the system is operating.

Top management at Food Co. still considers the system as one of their top priorities. One respondent affirms: "*Our CEO decided to invest in 4 fields: equipment, R&D, information systems, this means having always top notch IS and integration*". Top management always provided the necessary financial resources to improve the system and maximize its advantages. All respondents stressed the fact that there was never a blockage when it came to financial resources whether they were intended for global upgrades requiring considerable expenses (consultants, equipment, training, etc.), or for less costly system requirements (new modules, training, etc.). The VP of operations considers the top management's continuous willingness to invest and to always look for the added value of the system one of the main factors that has helped to assimilate the system. He says:

> "If I say for instance I would like to have such and such functionality and that it would cost us a consultant - knowing that their cost can reach $1000 or $2000 per day - I have never had to justify myself with reports and scientific studies...(Top management) willingness is always there…We have never had a blockage".

Moreover, top management takes part in the regular meetings of the ERP team where problems and new suggestions to improve the system are discussed and decisions are taken about the system.

At Plastic Co., things went quite differently. The ERP project was considered as part of a bigger enhancement project. At the time when the system was implemented, the CEO wanted to finish the project on time and within budget. The problem was that the people who were required to support the project (superusers-to-be) were not freed and their daily tasks were seen as more important than the project. This lack of commitment significantly delayed the project and negatively influenced the quality of the project. In 2006, the CEO changed as well as 6 VPs and 6 managers. The new CEO was determined to successfully lead and realize the project. One respondent reported that "*among the very first things that the new CEO said when he took his position is that they have spent about $3 or 4 million on JDE and that JDE is to stay and to operate successfully*".

Likewise, most of the new VPs already had experience with an ERP system and were sufficiently aware of its advantages and of the required sacrifice to make the project a success. As the VP of IT and project manager puts it:

> "I asked for resources, I had them…when I need people (to train) I don't have to ask 10 times to have a person. As a project manager, I talk to the VP and I tell him that we need to train this person for the system. Just one week later the person is freed up and he or she joins the training team to learn new things which are a prerequisite for a superuser".

3.2.4 Absorptive capacity

Several definitions have been suggested to identify absorptive capacity (ACAP). The most widely cited definition, however, is the one offered by Cohen and Levinthal (1990) who view the ACAP as the firm's ability to identify, acquire and assimilate new knowledge. A firm's absorptive capacity includes two main components: its prior relevant knowledge, and its investments in acquiring and assimilating new knowledge (Ravichandran 2005). Indeed, Szulanski (2000) argues that the availability of a pertinent knowledge in the organization doesn't necessarily mean its utilization in all the units of the organization.

When it comes to the first component, Food Co.'s system users can be classified in two major categories: those who are very interested in the system and who enjoy "*playing*" with it and even developing it, and those who are not very enthusiastic about it and who even, in some cases, avoid but still use its information for their daily activities. The first category generally includes most of the superusers and relatively young decision makers who feel comfortable with computers. The second group includes those who view the system as being made for the operations people and not for them. They were generally hostile to computers and preferred their old work methods. Nevertheless, the ERP team tried to indirectly integrate the second group into the system by pushing the information to them. In other words, instead of going into the system, looking for the required information, the reports they require are prepared for them and are presented in the format in which they are used.

As for the second component of the absorptive capacity (i.e., investments in acquiring new knowledge), Food Co. highly supports and encourages training and knowledge acquisition. The IT and ERP team members attend SAP and SAP users' conferences. Such events provide the team members with the opportunity to learn about new functionalities, about other experiences, meet the applications' developers, etc. When a new module is required, the firm seeks the help of consultants who work closely with the ERP team to implement the module.

At Plastic Co., the impact of the quality and the level of the absorptive capacity had a sharper impact. Overall, the level of computer literacy among users was low to average and users' reliance on the IT team was heavy. According to the VP of IT, those handicaps would have been limited if more time and resources had been allocated for training and education and appropriate system testing. He argues that the costs of errors, troubleshooting, extra time spent with users for support and the increased dependence of the latter on the IT people during the post-implementation stage could have been avoided if the go-live had been delayed by at least one month.

Another point that is worth noting concerning Plastic Co.'s absorptive capacity in general and its investment in acquiring and internalizing ERP knowledge in particular, is communication. According to a respondent, the information that users received about the system before its implementation was exaggerated and it reflected neither the limitations nor the real capabilities of the ERP system. Many managers and direct users were in fact disappointed with the system performance and outputs and were discouraged from further deploying the system.

3.2.5 Strategic alignment

For a long time, it has been argued that the strategic alignment between IT applications and strategy is associated with superior performance (Hirschheim and Sabherwal 2001; Somers and Nelson 2003). Somers and Nelson (2003) maintain that firms need to better integrate their business plans with their Information Systems in order to ensure the alignment of their information systems with the business strategy. Given the importance of ERP systems, firms need to successfully integrate and align their systems with their business strategy. Among other strategies, Somers and Nelson (2003) suggest organizational adaptation using business process reengineering and top management and user training and education, ERP alignment with strategy and assigning an ERP steering committee. ERP alignment with strategy could be done by placing some IT development resources under the control of a business unit and by ensuring that the system is perceived as strategically important to the firm. The ERP steering committee, on the other hand, would be responsible for making resource allocation decisions, providing organizational leadership and increasing and maintaining ERP visibility and coordination.

At Food Co., respondents assert that the system is perfectly supporting the firm's growth strategy. An ERP steering committee, including the top management, IT people and VPs, regularly meet to ensure that the system is aligned with its strategy and to evaluate the new needs and to make the required decisions about the system. If new modules or major updates are introduced, the necessary training and education sessions are organized for users. The continuous top management support and their involvement in all that concerns the ERP system in terms of development and improvement and the clear strategic vision that highlights the strategic importance of the ERP system for the firm's success are all indications of the appropriate alignment of the system with the firm's strategy.

The situation was quite different at Plastic Co. Before the arrival of the new CEO, the system's strategic importance for the firm was misunderstood. The system was primarily to serve the financial department's needs to centralize financial information. Both top management and managers lacked the appropriate understanding of the system's value and did not make the appropriate efforts to support the system and to promote its deployment. With the arrival of the new CEO and the new VPs, the system became among the top priorities of the firm's management. One respondent reported that *"among the very first things that the new CEO said when he took his position is that they have spent about $ 4 million on JDE and that JDE is to stay and to operate successfully"*. The IT team operates under the supervision of the finance department. This position allowed them to work closely with business managers and to properly meet their requirements.

3.2.6 User involvement

User involvement is strongly advocated in the IS literature as a means of increasing user satisfaction and acceptance of the system by developing realistic expectations about the system (Kumar et al. 2003; Markus et al. 2000). In fact, if the users' needs are ignored, the risk of resistance and rejection of the system increases and could result in personnel departure and high turnover (Kumar et al. 2003). In the case of ERP systems, taking into consideration the users' suggestions and feedback, along with effective education and efficient communication, could significantly improve the users' buy-in to the new system (Kawalek and Wood-Harper 2002).

Given that the system has been around for approximately 10 years, most of the users at Food Co. have adapted to the system. This is in addition to the fact that generally the people at Food Co., as one respondent asserted, are open to change and innovation. There are, however, some users who are willingly more involved with the system and with the superusers. They frequently contact the superusers to suggest and even make improvements, changes and extensions to the system.

> "They are the ones who are the most comfortable with computers. They are almost always the same ones who call us. Maybe because some are more interested than others and that they have a kind of network with the other users."

At Plastic Co., even though most of the users are becoming more comfortable with the system, there is still a lack of system buy-in in the company in general which is due to the lack of training and awareness about the system's capacities. The ERP/IT team, however, is presently making efforts to better educate high ranked managers about the system's progress, needs and capabilities. Similarly, the superusers are also continuously trained and informed about any new applications and features in the system, and they will in turn train users in their business unit.

3.2.7 Reward system

The link between reward strategies - such as rewarding the acquisition of new skills, linking compensation to company profits and other strategies - and learning improvement and the institutionalization of favorable behaviors has been established in the literature (Jerez-Gómez et al. 2005). Reward systems can also increase the retention rate of skilled employees and encourage further improvements at work.

In both companies, however, the reward system and the compensation system were not changed. According to one respondent at Food Co., the reason is that the "*for employees the change was not "harsh", their responsibility did not change and their regular tasks are unchanged, it's just that they are done better*". It is worth noting that there have been no departures at Food Co. since the system was implemented. At Plastic Co., however, there were some employee departures following the ERP system adoption. There is no evidence however, that this was due to the unchanged reward system. According to one respondent, this was mostly due to the frustration and rejection of the new system. Respondents at Plastic Co. also emphasized the issue of IT/ERP expertise turnover. They argued that incentives could be one effective solution to retain IT/ERP experts.

3.2.8 Institutional pressures

According to the Institutional Theory, organizations are influenced by their institutional environment and their decisions are made not only to increase their efficiency but also to legitimize themselves in their external environment (DiMaggio and Powell 1983; Scott 1995). Institutionalization occurs when organizations face several pressures (such as competing for resources, customers, political power, social and economic fitness) which push them to be isomorphic with respect to their environment (DiMaggio and Powell 1983; Teo et al. 2003). These pressures are described by DiMaggio and Powell (1983) as mimetic, coercive and normative forces.

Coercive pressures: Coercive pressures are the external pressures exerted by resource-dominant organizations (dominant suppliers and customers) and regulatory agencies and legislative bodies (DiMaggio and Powell 1983; Teo et al. 2003). As mentioned earlier in section 3.1, the system at Food Co. was primarily adopted in response to clients' pressures and requirements to provide quick, integrated and high quality information. Such coercive pressures are, in fact, permanent for Food Co. The superusers and the VP of IT admit that these pressures are "*obliging them to go further*" with the system by adopting new business processes and new functionalities. The firm had to adopt new business processes in order to satisfy the clients' requirements for product traceability, for example. Also, some of the clients recently demanded that Food Co. use Advanced Shipment Notices (ASN). This compelled the firm to integrate their license plates into their processes, which they had not done before. Food Co. on the other hand is not undergoing any pressure from its suppliers. Similarly, at Plastic Co. some of the clients have special requirements about quality and timeliness of exchanged data. Moreover, since the events of 9/11, new regulations were put in place by US customs which require detailed and timely reports and specific types of information. The ERP system helped Plastic Co. provide the required information on time and with the required detail.

Mimetic pressures: Mimetic pressures force firms, especially under conditions of uncertainty, to imitate other structurally equivalent firms, mainly successful ones (DiMaggio and Powell, 1983). As one of the leaders in the industry to implement an ERP system, Food Co. did not feel any mimetic pressures when they adopted the system. Nevertheless, as more and more competitors adopt the system, Food Co. feels that they "*lost what used to be a competitive advantage*". Possessing an ERP system is not prestigious anymore. Because of this, Food Co. realizes that it has no choice but to make the most out of the system and to take additional steps forward. As the VP of operations maintains:

> "(…) benefiting from all the advantages of all the functionalities is sure an advantage , but (we) also have to set off with innovations in this field…we have to be open to new functionalities .. (…).We should not be content by saying my system is stable… it is stable but it should move forward… so if we don't do that we will be outdistanced."

At Plastic Co., our respondents agreed that they were not undergoing any mimetic pressures. As the VP operations related:

> "If there is (mimetic) pressure, that would be our operational effectiveness which strongly pushes us to better assimilate the system…we have to

> improve in order to be competitive…by default we have to be better in order to cope with competition, no matter how our competitors arrive, we have to go."

Normative pressures: Normative pressures are exerted by professional communities and professional standards (DiMaggio and Powell 1983). Because of the evolutionary nature of ERP systems, normative pressures which tend to emerge through ERP user group communities, professional agencies, conferences, training and other professional events, could hardly be avoided. Indeed, Food Co. has already undergone two major upgrades which have been smoothly introduced. Moreover, new modules and functionalities are continuously being added. For Plastic Co., the system will soon be upgraded, but the respondents do not feel that normative pressures have had an impact on encouraging or hampering the assimilation of the system in their firm.

3.2.9 Vendor-consultant support

Several studies have shown that the long term relationship with the ERP vendor is essential for the system's success (Chang 2004; Somers and Nelson 2004). In the case of Food Co, the original vendor no longer exists and upgrades are bought from other vendors. Food Co. was however continuously up-to-date with system upgrades and innovations through SAP people, conferences, user groups, etc. When an upgrade or a new functionality needs to be installed, either the module vendor sends a consultant to help them with the installation or training, or they hire an independent consultant. The superusers work full time with the consultant. Then they take the responsibility of transferring the knowledge they acquire to the appropriate users. Having a few bad experiences with consultants at the time of the first major ERP implementation, the interviewees assert that a good choice of the consultant is one of the important factors for the proper assimilation of the system.

The situation at Plastic Co. is quite similar. The firm does not maintain a long term relationship with the vendor. A consulting firm leads the project, including business process reengineering, system installation and training. When the company needed to install new modules, a consultant was recruited. The consultants' expertise was also considered to be critical for the respondents, since they are responsible for knowledge transfer for both the IT team and the users.

The following table summarizes the findings concerning each of the factors that we examined in both companies:

	Food Co	Plastic Co
ERP attributes	• Flexibility • Perceived usefulness • Impact of other attributes diminished over time as the employees got used to the system	• Reliability • Ease of use • Accuracy • Flexibility • Perceived usefulness
IT expertise /user support	• Very competent • Appropriate support • ERP steering committee • Low turnover- high employee loyalty • Hot line for support • Night and evening shifts lack ERP support	• Very competent • Heavy workload • High ERP turnover • ERP steering committee • Hot line for support
Top management support and involvement	• Participates in person at ERP steering committee meetings • Provides the required financial support	• Clear strategic vision valuing ERP as an institutional tool for the firm • Doesn't participate in person at ERP meetings • Provides the required financial support
Absorptive capacity	• No previous experience with a similar system • Basic computer literacy • Training opportunities provided for IT/ ERP team • User training mainly during implementation and early post-implementation • No extra training for users	• No previous experience with a similar system • Basic computer literacy • Training opportunities provided for IT/ ERP team • Inappropriate user training and education
Strategic alignment	• ERP considered among the firm's priorities • ERP considered as an institutional tool for the firm's operational effectiveness • Regular post-implementation reviews	• ERP considered among the firm's priorities • Clear vision and business strategy that values the ERP as an important tool for the firm's operational effectiveness • Lack of understanding of the system's value among users • Post-implementation review of the project outcomes

	Food Co	Plastic Co
User involvement	• Operations manager highly involved with the system • ERP Steering committee open for suggestions and improvements of the system • Sales manager not involved	• Lack of trust in the system capabilities • News managers are supportive of the system • Liberates users when needed
Reward system	• No changes in reward system	• No changes in reward system • Could be a strategy to retain employees and ERP expertise and ERP knowledgeable IT members
Post-implementation vendor/consultant support	• No long term relationship with initial vendor • Requires vendor support for each implemented extension or module • No relationship with the initial vendor • Very important for knowledge transfer and training	• No relationship with the initial vendor • Requires vendor support for each implemented extension or module • Very important for knowledge transfer and training
Institutional pressures	• Mostly competitive (mimetic) pressures to stay in the lead • Normative pressures of other SAP adopters and professionals	• Mostly mimetic: pressures to maintain the leading position, • Government (customs) requirements to provide detailed high quality information
Assimilation	• Used for operational control • Used for management control • Firm's backbone • The core of SAP/3 is implemented and deployed • Managers use the system (direct contact with the system) except for the sales manager • New modules to extend and to improve the system (e.g. Business Warehouse)	• Used for operational control • Not all modules are implemented • Firm's backbone • To be implemented in the remaining plant • End-users mastering the basic functionalities of the system • Managers using the system outputs

Table 7- 3 Summary of findings

Conclusion

These case studies provide the following insights about ERP assimilation and its determinants of success.

• Size in terms of number employees seems to be advantageous for the smaller firm. With half the number of employees of Plastic Co., it was easier for Food Co. to manage its employees, to train its users and superusers and to educate managers about the system. This has in turn facilitated the assimilation process in the company and limited problems such as resistance to change and turnover.

• Both companies are similar, financially, at least in terms of revenues. Food Co. had the means to buy an expensive enterprise system, regularly extend and develop its system by introducing new modules with the assistance of consultants and provide its ERP people with the required training. Financial resources could be, therefore, considered as an indirect necessary, but not sufficient, determinant for improved assimilation.

• The longer the system is in the company, the better it is understood and the more the firm depends on it in its operations and decision-making processes.

• ERP attributes such as timeliness, accuracy, reliability, and flexibility are more attractive during the early stages of the project cycle. During the post-implementation stage, managers and users are aware of the system's capabilities, except in the case where new modules are introduced or training and education about the system were not adequate.

• IT skills and competence are important for ERP assimilation. Their presence is crucial to support managers and users, to maintain the system and to make the necessary system programming and development. When specific technical support is outsourced, close interaction with subcontractors is required in order to ensure IT-strategy alignment and efficient knowledge transfer.

• Top management championship remains a key factor for ERP assimilation. Their support is as important during implementation as it is during the post-implementation stage. They should understand the system and emphasize the importance of integration and cooperation across the firm. They should also establish rigorous rules about the use of parallel systems, as is the case at Plastic Co., in order to increase the project's efficiency and to speed up the system's benefits realization.

• Absorptive capacity is another important determinant for assimilation. Adequately training and educating users about the system, their tasks with regard to the system, and their business processes should be carefully planned according to the requirements of managers and users .

• The continuous evaluation of managers and users' skills and knowledge could avoid the costly and heavy dependence on IT personnel and would further improve their system's buy-in.

• The system and business strategy alignment is another requirement for assimilation. Indeed, the ERP system needs to support the strategy of each business unit in order to help managers in their decision-making processes.

• Considering managers' and users' feedback is another important determinant of successful system assimilation. For managers, being a member of the ERP steering committee helps build a sense of responsibility and of ownership in them which could improve their assimilation. Moreover, they would be more willing to liberate the required employees to participate in ERP team activities. One other important outcome of manager and user involvement is lower turnover and higher level of loyalty.

• A reward system does not seem to be critical for ERP assimilation. Once the system is integrated in the firm's business operations and becomes a necessity, users and managers have no choice but to use it and to depend on it.

• Coercive institutional pressures exerted by customers or by the government could influence the firm's assimilation and efforts to better deploy the system. When the firm is a leader in its industry, as was the case of Food Co. and Plastic Co., mimetic and normative forces have almost no impact on the firm's assimilation of its ERP system.

- A long term strategic relationship between the vendor and/or the consultant and the firm is not a requirement. When an upgrade or a new module is required, the firm shops for the product. The vendor could send a consultant to help the firm implement the module or it could simply hire an independent consultant who is specialized in that module.

These case studies may provide guidance to managers, IT professionals and consultants concerning the contextual factors which can be a positive influence on the realization of the desired benefits of ERP systems. They could also provide insight into the factors which are most problematic and most critical for the system's assimilation and long-term success in the organization.

CONCLUSION

Electronic communication media can help improve productivity and enhance competitiveness for both large and small firms. ICT can significantly reduce communication and coordination costs throughout firms' value chains, thereby improving the efficiency of operations. The chapters of this book suggest ICT have a significant impact on business processes, providing firms with new opportunities to undertake innovative projects, collaborate with other entities, test new ideas, share concepts and knowledge between the internal and external actors, and even bring innovations to the market. Smaller firms may have fewer incentives to integrate their business processes than larger firms, which have more complex business processes and resources to harmonize and coordinate. Moreover, most sectors are increasingly global and dominated by large firms but the structure of their value chains and operations shape opportunities for SMEs. The different ICT and e-business applications provide many benefits across a wide range of intra- and inter-firm business processes and transactions.

ICT can thus play a very important role because it can help SMEs both create business opportunities and combat pressures from competition. As we have seen in the preceding chapters of this book, appropriate ICT can help SMEs cut costs by improving their internal processes, improve their products through more rapid communication with their customers, and promote and distribute their products better via an online presence. To summarize, ICT has the potential to improve the core business of SMEs in every step of the business process. However, it must be noted at the outset that not all SMEs need to adopt ICT tools to the same degree of sophistication or invest in it at the same level. Even if SMEs are increasingly aware of the benefits of ICT, they will only adopt them if they can overcome a number of barriers.

As we have illustrated in this book, use of and investment in ICT requires complementary investments in skills, organization, innovation and investment. This change entails risks and costs as well as bringing potential benefits. SMEs generally lack the human technological resources needed for ICT and e-commerce because they focus on day-to-day operations and lack the time to understand the benefits of new technologies. Even when they are aware of the potential benefits of adopting e-commerce, they require know-how or qualified personnel. SMEs may also lack managerial understanding and skills for e-business. Successful integration of e-business requires many firms to restructure their business processes, to change organizational structures and to redefine their core competences and positions in the value chains. The strategic challenge is thus not only to make the technological investment, but also to redefine the processes and skills in place in the company so the technology can be implemented effectively.

SMEs may lack objective information regarding the benefits and costs of adopting ICT. The private sector, the trade associations and government each have a role, and can provide information about available services and, when necessary, improve coordination of government information about the benefits of adoption and use of ICT. Governments have an important obligation to ensure that adequate policies and initiatives are in place and enabling environments are created to encourage the adoption of ICT in SMEs. Policy initiatives in some cases aim at facilitating SME participation in product and sector value chains and providing them with information to assess the opportunities and costs of ICT.

Governments have used many policies to encourage e-business and Internet use, from fostering technological diffusion to creating a favorable business environment with fair and predictable rules. However, there is no one-size-fits all approach to policy, and the policy mix and priorities will depend on national circumstances (leading or lagging countries) and sectorial distribution of economic activity, as well as size factors. More research is also needed to understand the possible supporting role of trade associations in facilitating small supplier involvement in relational exchange and electronic communications technology. There may be a role for small business trade associations in providing affordable ICT training and support on a group basis.

ICT provides SMEs with opportunities to participate in new supply chains and markets. Nevertheless, the improvement in competitiveness is not the result of ICT *per se*, but of the combination of ICT features with organizational arrangements and practices that support their use. Firms and ICT are designed, but given their complexity and interaction, the results are mutable and dynamic. Complementary investments in skills, organizational change and innovation are the keys to making ICT work to a company's advantage. The use of ICT affects firms' performance, primarily when accompanied by other changes and investments. Without these, the economic impact of ICT may be limited. In order to ensure successful ICT adoption, SMEs will have to carefully consider which ICT will best fit their strategic and organizational goals, management structures and customers.

Even if most SMEs lack managerial expertise and tend to pursue less aggressive strategic options than large firms, the preceding chapters illustrate different examples of ICT use by SMEs to improve their business processes. ICT forms one of the three legs of contingency theory as a determinant of organizational structure, along with organizational size and organization and the environment. Innovations in ICT create new options, raising new questions to explore, especially for SMEs. For example, Web 2.0 applications that bring collective wisdom to the fore can also uncover potential business innovations, particularly for firms with limited resources. These kinds of technologies are changing the ways firms do business. In this book, we presented a synthesis of the challenges and opportunities of using ICT in SMEs. It is clear that many issues remain to be explored, providing fertile ground for future research.

REFERENCES

Addison, T. 2003. E-commerce project development risks: evidence from a Delphi survey. *International Journal of Information Management*, 23(1): 25-40.

Ahituv, N., S. Neumann, and M. Zviran. 2002. A system development methodology for ERP systems. *Journal of Computer Information systems*, 42(3):56-67.

Alavi, M., and D. E. Leidner. 2001. Review: knowledge management and knowledge management systems: conceptual foundations and research issues. *MIS Quarterly*, 25(1): 107-136.

Amoako-Gyampah, K., and A. F. Salam. 2004. An extension of the technology acceptance model in an ERP implementation environment. *Information & Management*, 41(6): 731-745.

Anthony, T. 2000. Supply chain collaboration: success in the New Internet Economy. In T. Anthony (Ed.), *Achieving supply chain excellence through technology,* San Francisco, CA: Montgomery Research Inc., 41-44.

Antonelli. C. 1986. The international diffusion of new information technologies. *Research Policy, Elsevier*, 15(3):139-147.

Armstrong, C., and V. Sambamurthy. 1999. Information technology assimilation in firms: the influence of senior leadership and IT infrastructures. *Information systems research*, 10(4): 304-32.

Asproth, V., and C.A. Nystrôm. 2008. Communication and information exchange among SMEs and their local environment. *Journal of Organisational Transformation & Social Change*, 5(2): 175-189.

Atrostic, B., and R. Jarmin. 2003. IT and economic performance: evidence from micro data studies. In *Digital Economy 2003.* Economics And Statistics Administration, U.S. Department of Commerce. December 2003, 61-80.

Azouzi, R., R. Beauregard, and S. D'Amours. 2007. *A Typology Integrating Advanced Manufacturing Technologies and Customization Strategies in Furniture Manufacturing. Innovative Processes and Products for Mass Customization.* Blecker T., Edwards K., Friedrich G., Hvam L., Salvador F. (Eds.), Berlin: GITO-Verlag, Series on Business Informatics and Application Systems, Vol. 3, 23-38.

Baets, W. 1992. Aligning information systems with business strategy. *IS and business strategy alignment*, 1(4): 205-213.

Bajwa, D., J.E. Garcia, and T. Mooney. 2004. An integrative framework for the assimilation of enterprise resource planning systems: phases, antecedents, and outcomes. *Journal of Computer Information Systems*, 44(3): 81-90.

Baldwin, J.R., D. Sabourin. 2002. *Impact of the Adoption of Advanced ICTs on Firm Performance in the Canadian Manufacturing Sector*, STI Working Papers 2002/1, OECD, Paris

Barba Sanchez, V., M. Del Pilar Martinez-Ruiz, and A. Jimenez-Zarco. 2007. Divers benefits and challenges of ICT adoption by small and medium enterprises: a litterature review. *Problems and Perspectives in Management*, 5(1): 103-114.

Barker, T., and M. N. Frolick. 2003. ERP implementation failure: A case study. *Information Systems Management*, 20(4): 43-49.

Barrett, S., and B. Konsynski. 1982. Inter-organization information sharing systems. *MIS Quarterly*, 6: 93-105

Beard, J.W., and M. Sumner. 2004. Seeking strategic advantage in the post-net era: Viewing ERP systems from the resource-based perspective. *The Journal of Strategic Information Systems*, 13(2): 129-150.

Beckinsale, M., M. Levy, and P. Powell. 2007. Exploring internet adoption drivers in SMEs. *Electronic Markets*, 16(4): 361-370.

Benbya, H., and B. McKelvey. 2006. Using coevolutionary and complexity theories to improve IS alignment: a multi-level approach. *Journal of Information Technology*, 21(4): 284-298.

Bendixen, M., K. A. Bukasa, and R. Abratt. 2004. Brand equity in the business-to-business market. *Industrial Marketing Management*, 33(5): 371-380.

Bensaou, M., and N. Venkatraman. 1996. Inter-organizational relationship and information technology: a conceptual synthesis and a research framework. *European Journal of Information Systems*, *5(2)*: 84-91.

Bergeron, F., L. Raymond, and S. Rivard. 2004. Ideal patterns of strategic alignment and business performance. *Information & Management*, 41(8): 1003-1020.

Bergeron, F., L. Raymond, and S. Rivard. 2001. Fit in strategic information technology management research: an empirical comparison of perspectives. *Omega*, 29(2): 125-142.

Bergeron, F., and L. Raymond. 1995. The contribution of IT to the bottom line: a contingency perspective of strategic dimensions. Paper presented at the 16th International Conference on Information Systems, December 13-15, in Amsterdam, Netherlands. *Proceeding of the 16th International Conference on Information Systems*, 167-181.

Bergstrom, M., and L. Stehn. 2005. Matching industrialised timber frame housing needs and enterprise resource planning: A change process. *International Journal of Production Economics*, 97(2): 172-184.

Bermudez, P. Z., M. A. A., Turkman, and K. F. Turkman. 2001. *A predictive approach to tail probability estimation*, Boston: Extremes, 4(4): 295-315.

Bhagwat, R., and M. K. Sharma. 2007. Information system architecture: a framework for a cluster of small and medium-sized enterprises (SMEs). *Production Planning and Control*, 18(4): 283-298.

Botta-Genoulaz, V., P-A. Millet, and B. Grabot. 2005. A survey on the recent research literature on ERP systems. *Computers in Industry*, 56(6): 510-522.

Bowles, M., and P. Wilson. 2002. Why ICT and economic growth requires deliberate effort to accelerate SME adoption and deployment of IT and e-commerce. Position Paper, Australian Electronic Commerce Centre.

Bradley, L., and K. Stewart. 2003. A Delphi study of internet banking. *Marketing Intelligence & Planning*, 21(5): 272-281.

Breu, K., and J. Peppard. 2003. Useful knowledge for information system practice: the contribution of the participatory paradigm. *Journal of Information Technology*, 18(3): 177-195.

Bruque, S., S. Ruque, and J. Moyano. 2007. Organisational determinants of information technology adoption and implementation in SMEs: The case of family and cooperative firms. *Technovation*, 27(5): 241-253.

Brynjolfsson, E., A. A. Renshaw, and M. Van Alstyne. 1997. The matrix of change. *Sloan Management Review*, 38(2): 22-40.

Bucar, M., M. Stare, and A. Jaklic. 2006. eStrategy and ICT investment in Slovenia. Paper presented at the 19th Bled eConference eValues, June 5-7, in Bled, Slovenia. *BLED 2006 Proceedings*. Paper 19.

Burke, K. 2005. The Impact of Firm Size on Internet Use in Small Business. *Electonic Markets*, 15(2): 79-93.

Burn, J.M., and C. Szeto. 2000. A comparison of the views of business and IT management on success factors for strategic alignment. *Information & Management*, 37(4): 197-216.

Byrd, A., B. R. Lewis, and R.W. Bryan. 2006. The leveraging influence of strategic alignment on IT investment: an empirical examination. *Information & Management*, 43(3): 308-321.

Cabaniss, K. 2001. Counselling and computer technology in the new millennium – an internet Delphi study. PhD Diss., Virginia Polytechnic Institute and State University.

Caisse, S., and B. Montreuil. 2009. Exploiting a Business Design Framework for Modeling Multi-Stakeholder Business Relationships.

Frontiers of E-Business Research 2009. CD-ROM ed. Finland: Tampere University of Technology and University of Jyväskylä.

Caisse, S. 2008. Tetrahedral business design framework. PhD Diss., Université Laval, Quebec, Canada.

Caisse, S., and B. Montreuil. 2005. Conceptualizing business in the new economy. Paper presented at the Frontiers of E-Business Research 2005. September 2005, in Tampere, Finland. *Proceedings of Frontiers of E-Business Research*, 786-800.

Caisse, S., and B. Montreuil. 2002. Towards an e-business design framework. Paper presented at the Frontiers of E-Business Research 2002. November 2002, in Tampere, Finland. *Proceedings of Frontiers of E-business Research*, 93-106.

Caldeira, M. M., and J. M. Ward. 2003. Using resource-based theory to interpret the successful adoption and use of information systems and technology in manufacturing small and medium-sized enterprise. *European Journal of Information Systems*, 12(2): 127-142.

Canadian eBusiness initiative. 2004. Net Impact Canada IV: Strategies for increasing SME engagement in the e-economy. Industry Canada.

Canetta, L., N. Cheikhrouhou, and R. Glardon. 2007. A rule-based DSS for the qualitative prediction of the evolution of e-sales. Paper presented at the Third International Conference on Web Information Systems and Technologies for the Society e-Business and e-Government / e-Learning, in Barcelona, Spain. *Proceedings of WEBIST*, 97-106.

Canetta, L., N. Cheikhrouhou, R. Glardon, and N. Iliev. 2004. Supporting electronic sales channels deployment through the analysis of customer preferences. Paper presented at the IEEE Conference on Systems, Man and Cybernetics, in Den Haag, Netherlands. *Proceedings of IEEE Conference on Systems, Man and Cybernetics,* 4123-4128.

Carr, N. 2003. "IT doesn't matter." *Harvard Business Review*, 81(5): 41-49.

Cassivi, L. 2006. Collaboration planning in a supply chain. *Supply Chain Management: An International Journal*, 11(3): 249-258.

Cassivi, L., E. Lefebvre, L. A. Lefebvre, and P.-M. Léger. 2004. Supply chain planning and execution tools: E-collaboration and organizational performance. *International Journal of Logistics Management*, 15(1): 91-110.

Cattell, K.S. 2002. Foresight, space and e-commerce. *Facilities*, 20(3/4):145-162.

Centre francophone d'informatisation des organisations (Cefrio). 2005. Pour une utilisation plus efficace des technologies de l'information. Avis présenté au Ministère du Développement économique, de l'Innovation et de l'Exportation (MDEIE), Gouvernement du Québec, Canada.

European Committee for Standardization. CEN Workshop Agreement. 2004. European guide to good practice in knowledge management – Part 3: SME Implementation. *CWA,* 1(49): 24-3.

Cegarra-Navarro, J.G., D. Jimenez, and E.A. Martinez-Conesa. 2007. Implementing e-business through organizational learning: An empirical investigation in SMEs. *International Journal of Information Management,* 27(3): 173-186.

Chan, K.W., and R. A. Mauborgne. 1997. Value innovation: The strategic logic for high growth. *Harvard Business Review,* 75(1): 102-112.

Chan, M .F. S., K. F. Keung, and W. W. C. Chung. 2000. A design of an ABC template for easy assimilation in SME. *Logistics Information Management*, 13(3): 126-137.

Chan, Y. E., and B. H. Reich. 2007. IT alignment: what have we learned? *Journal of Information Technology*, 22(4): 297-315.

Chan, Y. E., R. Sabherwal, and J. B. Thatcher. 2006. Antecedents and outcomes of strategic IS alignment: an empirical investigation. *IEEE Transactions on Engineering Management*, 51(3): 27-47.

Chan, Y. E., and S. L. Huff. 1993. Investigating information systems strategic alignment. Paper presented at the Fourteenth International Conference on Information Systems, Orlando, USA. *Proceedings of Fourteenth International Conference on Information Systems*, 345-363.

Chang, H-L, and S-H. Chen. 2005. Assessing the readiness of internet-based IOS and evaluating its impact on adoption. Paper presented at the 38th Annual International Hawaii Conference of Systems Sciences, January 3-6, in Hawaii. *Proceedings of the 38th Annual Hawaii International Conference on System Sciences* – 2005, track 7.

Chang, S. 2004. ERP life cycle implementation, management and support: implications for practice and research. Paper presented at the 37th Annual Hawaii International Conference on System Sciences, January 5-8, in Hawaii. *Proceedings of the 37th Annual Hawaii International Conference on System Sciences*, track 8.

Chatterjee, D., R. Grewal, and V. Sambamurthy. 2002. Shaping Up for e-commerce: institutional enablers of the organizational assimilation of Web technologies. *MIS Quarterly*, 26(2): 65-89.

Chen, F. 1999. Decentralized supply chains subject to information delays. *Management Science*, 45: 1076-1090.

Chen, M.T. 2000. Selecting the right engineer, contractor, and Supplier. *AACE International Transactions*. P7A.

Chen, R. S., C. M. Sun, M. M. Helms, and K. Jih. 2008. Aligning information technology and business strategy with a dynamic capabilities perspective: a longitudinal study of a Taiwanese semiconductor company. *International Journal of Information Management,* 28(5): 366-378.

Chen, R. S., C. M. Sun, M. M. Helms, and K. Jih. 2008. Role Negotiation and Interaction: An Exploratory Case Study of the Impact of Management Consultants on ERP System Implementation in SMEs in Taiwan. *Information Systems Management*, 25(2): 159-173.

Chesbrough, H. 2007. Business model innovation: It's not just about technology anymore. *Strategy & Leadership*, 35(6): 12-17.

Chien, S-W., C. Hu, K. Reimers, and J-S. Lin. 2007. The influence of centrifugal and centripetal forces on ERP project success in small and medium-sized enterprises in China and Taiwan. *International Journal of Production Economics*, 107(2): 380-396.

Choi, B., C. Lee, H. Lee, and M. Subramani. 2004. Effects of Web retail service quality and product Categories on Consumer Behavior. Paper presented at the 37th Annual Hawaii International Conference on System Sciences (HICSS), January 5-8, in Hawaii. *Proceedings of the 37th Annual Hawaii International Conference on System Sciences*, track 7.

Chopra, S., D. Dougan, and G. Taylor. 2001. B2B e-commerce opportunities. *Supply Chain Management Review*, 5(3): 50-58.

Choudhury, V. 1997. Strategic choices in the development of interorganizational information systems. *Information Systems Research*, 8(1): 1-24.

Christensen, C. M., and J. L. Bower. 1996. Customer power, strategic investment, and the failure of leading firms. *Strategic Management Journal*, 17(3): 197-218.

Christy, D. P., and J. R. Grout. 1994. Safeguarding supply chain relationships. *International Journal of Production Economics*, 36(3): 233-242.

Clemons, E.K., and R. Aron. 2002. Online distribution: a taxonomy of channel structures determinants of outcome and determinants of strategy. Paper presented at the 35th Annual on System Science (HICSS), January 7-10, in Hawaii. *Proceedings of the 35th Annual Hawaii International Conference on System Science*, 2330-2339.

Cohen, W., and D. Levinthal. 1990. Absorptive capacity: a new perspective on learning and innovation. *Administrative Science Quarterly*, 35(1): 128-152.

Conner, K. R., and C. K. Prahalad. 1996. A resource-based theory of the firm: knowledge versus opportunism. *Organization Science*, 7(5): 477-501.

Cooper, R. B., and R. W. Zmud. 1990. Information technology implementation research: a technological diffusion approach. *Management Science*, 36(2): 123-139.

Corso, M., A., Martini, E. Paolucci, and L. Pellegrini. 2003. Knowledge management configurations in Italian small-to-medium enterprises. *Integrated Manufacturing Systems*, 14(1): 46-56.

Côté, L., M. Vézina, and V. Sabourin. 2005. The strategic management process in e-business. *Ivey Business Journal Online* May-June 2005, Vol. 69, N 5, 1-7.

Cragg, P. B., and M. King. 1993. Small-firm computing: motivators and inhibitors. *MIS Quarterly,* 17(1): 47-60.

Croteau, A.-M., P.-M. Léger, and L. Cassivi. 2007. The role of life cycle concepts in the assessment of interorganizational alignment. *Industrial Management & Data*, 108(2): 145-161.

Croteau, A.-M., and F. Bergeron. 2001. An information technology trilogy: business strategy, technological deployment and organization performance. *Journal of Strategic Information Systems*, 10(2): 77-99.

Damsgaard, J., and K. Lyytinen. 1996. Government strategies to promote the diffusion of electronic data interchange (EDI): What we know and what we don't know. *Information Infrastructure and Policy*, 5: 169-190.

Da Silveira, G.J.C., and R. Cagliano. 2006. The relationship between interorganizational information systems and operations performance. *International Journal of Operations & Production Management*, 26(3): 232-253.

Davenport, T.H. 1998. Putting the enterprise into the enterprise system. *Harvard Business Review,* 76(4): 121-131.

Davis, F.D. 1989. Perceived usefulness, perceived ease of use, and user acceptance of information technology. *MIS Quarterly*, 13(3): 319-340.

De Burca, S., B. Fynes, and D. Marshall. 2005. Strategic technology adoption: extending ERP across the supply-chain. *Journal of Enterprise Information Management*, 18(4): 427-440.

DeLone, W. H., and E. R. McLean. 2002. Information systems success: the quest for the dependent Variable(s) Revisited. Paper presented at the 35th Annual Hawaii International Conference on System Sciences, January 7-10, in Hawaii. *Proceedings of the 35th Annual Hawaii International Conference on System Sciences*, 2966-2976.

D'Este, P., and P. Patel. 2007. University-industry linkages in the UK: what are the factors underlying the variety of interactions with industry? *Research Policy*, 36(9): 1295-1313.

Dillman, D. A. 2000. *Mail and internet surveys: the tailored design method.* New York: John Wiley.

DiMaggio, P J., and W. W. Powell.1983. The iron cage revisited: institutional isomorphism and collective rationality in organizational fields. *American Sociological Review*, 48(2): 147-160.

Disney, S. M., and D. R. Towill. 2003. Bullwhip reduction in supply chains: the impact of VMI. *International Journal of Operations and Production Management*, 23 (5/6): 625-651.

Dixon, T., B. Thompson, and P. McAllister. 2002. The value of ICT for SMEs in the UK: A critical literature review. Report for Small Business Service Research Program. The College of Estate Management.

Dowlatshahi, S. 2005. Strategic success factors in enterprise resource planning design and implementation: A Case Study Approach. *International Journal of Production Research*, 43(18): 3754-3771.

Downs, G. W., and L. B. Mohr. 1976. Conceptual issues in the study of innovation. *Administrative Science Quarterly*, 21(4): 700-714.

Drazin, R., and A. H. Van de Ven. 1985. An examination of the alternative forms of contingency theory. *Administrative Science Quarterly*, 30(4): 514-539.

Eikebrokk, T. R., and D. H. Olsen. 2007. An empirical investigation of competency factors affecting e-business success in European SMEs. *Information & Management*, 44(4): 364-383.

Eisenhardt, K. 1989. Building theories from case study research. *The Academy of Management Review*, 14(4): 532-550.

Eisenhardt, K., and M. Graebner. 2007. Theory building from cases: opportunities and challenges. *Academy of Management Journal*, 50(1): 25-32.

Elgarah, W. N., Falaleeva, C. S. Saunders, V. Ilie, J. T. Shim, and J. F. Courtney. 2005. Data Exchange in Interorganizational Relationships: Review through Multiple Conceptual lenses[1]. Database for Advances in Information Systems, 36(1): 8-29.

Elia, E., L. A. Lefebvre, and E. Lefebvre. 2007. Focus of B-to-B e-commerce initiatives and related benefits in manufacturing small and medium-sized enterprises. *Information Systems and eBusiness Management*, 5(1): 1-24.

Esselaar, S., C. Stork, A. Ndiwalana, and M. Deen-Swarray. 2007. ICT Usage and Its Impact on Profitability of SMEs in 13 African Countries. *Information Technologies & International Development*, 4(1): 87-100.

Etzkowitz, H. 2003. Innovation in innovation: the triple helix of university-industry-government Relations. *Studies of Science*, 42(3): 293-337.

Etzkowitz, H., and L. Leydesdorff. 2000. The dynamics of innovation: from national systems and 'Mode 2' to a triple helix of university-industry-government relations. *Research Policy*, 29(2): 109-123.

Ewton, S.E. 2003. Assessment of the impacts of e-commerce technologies on overall business processes an analytic Delphi process. Paper presented at the Portland International Conference on Management of Engineering and Technology (PICMET'03), July 20-24, in Portland, USA.

Fawcett, S. E., and G. M. Magnan. 2004. Ten guiding principles for high-impact SCM. *Business Horizons*, 47(5): 67-74.

Featherman, M. S., and J. D. Wells. 2004. The intangibility of e-services: effects on artificiality, perceived risk, and adoption. Paper presented at the 37th Annual Hawaii International Conference on System Science (HICSS). January 5-8, in Hawaii. *Proceedings of the 37th Annual Hawaii International Conference on System Science,* 177-187.

Fichman, R. G. 2000. The diffusion and assimilation of information technology innovations. In the *Framing the domains of IT management: Projecting the future ... through the past*, R. W. Zmud (Ed.), Cincinnati, OH: Pinnaflex Educational Resources Inc., 105-128.

Fichman, R. G., and C. F. Kemerer. 1997. The assimilation of software process innovations: an organizational learning perspective. *Management Science*, 43(10): 1345-1363.

Fichman, R. G., and C. F. Kemerer. 1993. Adoption of software engineering process innovations: the case of object orientation. *Sloan Management Review*, 30: 47-59.

Fillis, I., U. Johansson, and B. Wagner. 2003. A conceptualization of the opportunities and barriers to e-business development in the smaller firm. *Journal of Small Business and Enterprise Development*, 10(3): 336-344.

Fisher, M. L. 1997. What is the right supply chain for your product? *Harvard Business Review*, 75(2): 105-116.

Foreman-Peck, J., G. Makepeace, and B. Morgan 2006. Growth and profitability of small and medium-sized enterprises: Some Welsh evidence. *Regional Studies*, 40(4): 307-319.

Foster, R. 1986. "*Innovation: The Attacker's Advantage*." New York: Summit Books.

Frazier, G. L., and R. C. Rody. 1991. The use of influence strategies in interfirm relationships in industrial product channels. *Journal of Marketing*, 55(1): 52-69.

Ganesan, S. 1994. Determinants of long-term orientation in buyer-seller relationships. *Journal of Marketing*, 58(2): 1-19.

Gatignon, H., T. S. Robertson. 1989. Technology diffusion: an empirical test of competitive effects. *Journal of Marketing*, 53(1): 35-49.

Gefen, D. 2003. Assessing unidimensionality through Lisrel: an explanation and example. *Communications of the Association for Information Systems*, 12: 23-47.

Gopalakrishnan, S., and M. D. Santoro. 2004. Distinguishing between knowledge transfer and technology transfer activities: the role of key organizational factors. *IEEE Transactions on Engineering Management*, 51(1): 57-69.

Goshal, S., and C. Bartlett. 1997. *The individualized corporation: A Fundamental New Approach to Management*. New York: HarperBusiness.

Grandon, E. E., and J. M. Pearson. 2004. Electronic commerce adoption: an empirical study of small and medium US businesses. *Information and Management,* 42(1): 197-216.

Greene, W. H. 1997. *Econometric analysis.* 3rd. ed. Upper Saddle River, NJ: Prentice-Hall.

Griffy-Brown, C., and M. Chun. 2007. Aligning business strategy and IS resources in Japanese SMEs: A resource-based view. *Journal of Global Information Technology Management*, 10(3): 28-51.

Grover, V. 1993. An empirical derived model for the adoption of customer-based interorganizational systems. *Decision Sciences*, 24(3): 603-640.

Gupta, M., and A. Kohli. 2006. Enterprise resource planning systems and its implications for operations management. *Technovation*, 26(5-6): 687-696.

Gurunlian, J., and L. Zhongzhou. 2001. E-commerce and development report. United Nations Conference on Trade and Development. New York and Geneva: United Nations Publications.

Hadaya, P. 2004. Les déterminants de la stratégie de commerce électronique poursuivie par les entreprises canadiennes. Ph.D diss., École Polytechnique de Montréal, Canada.

Hair, J. F., R. E. Anderson, and R. L. Tatham. 1998. *Multivariate Data Analysis*, 5th ed. New Jersey: Prentice Hall.

Hamel, G. 2000. *Leading the revolution.* Boston: Harvard Business School Press.

Hamill, J., K. Gregory. 1997. Internet marketing in the internationalization of UK SMEs. *Journal of Marketing Management*, 13(1): 9-28.

Hart, P. J., and C. S. Saunders. 1997. Power and trust: critical factors in the adoption and use of electronic data interchange. *Organization Science*, 8: 23-42.

Hassanein, K., and M. Head. 2004. The influence of product type on on-line trust. Paper presented at the 17th Bled Electronic Commerce Conference, June 21-23, in Bled, Slovenia.

Henderson, J. C., and N. Venkatraman. 1993. Strategic alignment: leveraging information technology for transforming organizations. *IBM Systems Journal*, 32(1): 4-16.

Henderson, J. C., and N. Venkatraman. 1991. Understanding strategic alignment. *Business Quaterly,* 55(3): 72-79.

Hirschheim, R., and R. Sabherwal. 2001. Detours in the path toward strategic information systems alignment. *California Management Review*, 44(1): 87-108.

Ho, D. C. K., K. F. Au, and N. Edward. 2003. The process and consequences of supply chain virtualization. *Industrial Management + Data Systems*, 103 (5/6): 423-433.

Holmberg, S. C. 2001. Taking Syntegrity-4 from Assumption Mode to Reflection Mode. *Systems Research and Behavioral Science*, 18 (2): 127-135.

Holzmuller, H. H., and J. Schluchter. 2002. Delphi study about the future of B2B marketplaces in Germany. *Electronic Commerce Research and Applications*, 1: 2-19.

Hong, I. B. 2002. A new framework for interorganizational systems based on the linkage of participants' roles. *Information & Management*, 39(4): 261-270.

Hua, G. B. 2007. Applying the strategic alignment model to business and ICT strategies of Singapore's small and medium-sized architecture, engineering and construction enterprises. *Construction Management and Economics*, 25(2): 157-169.

Huang, J., H. Wang, and C. Zhao. 2005. E-commerce success factors: exploratory and empirical research on the Chinese publishing industry. Paper presented at the 2005 IEEE International Conference on e-Business Engineering (ICEBE'05), October 12-18, Beijing, China. *Proceedings of 2005 IEEE International Conference on e-Business Engineering*, 465-472.

Hunter, L. M., C. J. Kasouf, K. J. Celuch, and K. A. Curry. 2004. A classification of business-to-business buying decisions: risk importance and probability as a framework for e-business benefits. *Industrial Marketing Management*, 33(2): 145-154.

Hunt, S. D., D. B. Arnett, and S. Madhavaram. 2006. The explanatory foundations of relationship marketing theory. *The Journal of Business and Industrial Marketing*, 21(2): 72.

Hyjek, M., and J. Sharp. 2006. *Does ICT matter to SMBs in Canada?* Canadian Small and Medium Business Markets: Special Study. IDC Vol.1.

Iacovou, C. L., I. Benbasat, and A. S. Dexter. 1995. Electronic data interchange and small organizations: adoption and impact of technology. *MIS Quarterly*, 19:465-486.

Ifinedo, P. 2007. Interactions between organizational size, culture and structure and some IT factors in the context of ERP success assessment: an exploratory investigation. *The Journal of Computer Information Systems*, 47(4): 28-41.

Iliev, N., R. Alard, L. Canetta, and N. Cheikhrouhou. 2004. Evaluating electronic enabled transaction costs´ efficiency. Proceedings of International Paper presented at the Global Production Management, September 6-8, in Bandung, Indonesia. *Proceedings of the Global Production Management,* 21-31.

Ilsoon, S. 2006. Adoption of enterprise application software and firm performance. *Small Business Economics,* 26(3): 241-256.

Iskanius, P., and H. Kilpala. 2006. One step closer towards e-business – the implementation of a supporting ICT system. *International Journal of Logistics: Research and Applications*, 9(3): 283-293.

Ismail, N. A., and M. King. 2006. The alignment of accounting and information systems in SMEs in Malaysia. *Journal of Global Information Technology Management*, 9(3): 24-42.

Jansen-Vullers, M. H., M. Netjes, and H. A. Reijers. 2004. Business process redesign for effective e-commerce. Paper presented at the 6th International Conference on Electronic Commerce, October 25-27, in Delft, Netherlands. *Proceedings of the 6th International Conference on Electronic Commerce,* ACM International Conference Proceeding Series; Vol. 60: 382-391.

Jasperson, J., P. F. Carter, and R. W. Zmud. 2005. A comprehensive conceptualization of the post-adoptive behaviors associated with it-enabled work systems. *MIS Quarterly*, 29(3): 525-557.

Jeon, B. N., K. S. Han, and M. J. Lee. 2006. Determining factors for the adoption of e-business: the case of SMEs in Korea. *Applied Economics*, (38, 16): 1905-1916.

Jerez-Gómez, P., J. Céspedes-Lorente, and R. Valle-Cabrera. 2005. Organizational learning and compensation strategies: evidence from the Spanish chemical industry. *Human Resource Management*, 44(3): 279-299.

Johnson, E., S. Whang. 2002. E-business and supply chain management: an overview and framework. *Production and Operations Management*, 11: 413-423.

Johnston, K., S. Jiwei, Z. Dann, and I. Barcay. 2006. Knowledge, power and trust in SME *e*-based virtual organizations. *International Journal of Networking & Virtual Organisations*, 3(1): 42-59.

Johnston, H. R., and M. R. Vitale. 1988. Creating competitive advantage with interorganizational information systems. *MIS Quarterly*, 12(2): 153-165.

Jones, M. C. 2005. Tacit knowledge sharing during ERP implementation: a multi-site case study. *Information Resources Management Journal*, 18(2): 1-23.

Kawalek, P., and T. Wood-Harper. 2002. The finding of Thorns: user participation in enterprise systems implementation. *The Database for Advances in Information Systems*, 33(1): 13-21.

Kefi, H., and M. Kalika. 2005. Survey of Strategic Alignment Impacts on Organizational Performance in International European companies. Paper presented at the 38[Th] Annual Hawaii International Conference on System Sciences (HICSS), January 3-6, Hawaii. *Proceedings of the 38th Annual International Hawaii Conference on System Sciences*, 230c.

Kendall, J. D., L. L. Tung, K. H. Chua, NG, C. Hong, NG. Dennis, and S. M. Tan. 2001. Receptivity of Singapore's SMEs to Electronic Commerce Adoption. *Journal of Strategic Information Systems*, 10: 223-242.

Kersten, W., K. A. Schroeder, and A. Schulte-Bisping. 2004. Internet-Supported Sourcing of Complex Materials. *Business Process Management Journal*, 10: 101-114.

Kiang, M. Y., T. S. Raghu, and K. H. M. Shang. 2000. Marketing on the internet - who can benefit from an online marketing approach? *Decision Support Systems*, 27: 383-393.

Ko, D. G., L. J. Kirsch, and W. R. King. 2005. Antecedents of knowledge transfer from consultants to clients in enterprise system implementation. *MIS Quarterly*, 29(1): 59-78.

Koh, S. C. L., and M. Simpson. 2005. Change and uncertainty in SME manufacturing environments using ERP. *Journal of Manufacturing Technology Management*, 16(5/6): 629-654.

Kremic, T. 2003. Technology transfer: A contextual approach. *Journal of Technology Transfer*, 28: 149-158.

Kumar, K., and H. G. van Dissel. 1996. Sustainable collaboration: managing conflict and cooperation in inter-organizational systems. *MIS Quarterly*, 20(3): 279-300.

Kumar, V., B. Maheshwari, and U. Kumar. 2003. An investigation of critical management issues in ERP implementation: empirical evidence from Canadian organizations. *Technovation*, 23(9): 793-807.

Lambert, D. M., M. A. Emmelhainz, and J. T. Gardner. 1999. Building successful partnerships. *Journal of Business Logistics*, 20: 165-181.

Lawson-Body, A., A. Illia, and J. Jimenez. 2006. Impact of date integration on CRM in the electronic commerce of SMEs. *Academy of Information and Management Sciences Journal*, 9(1): 83-103.

Lee, T-R, and J-M. Li. 2006. Key factors in forming an e-marketplace: an empirical analysis. *Electronic Commerce Research and Applications*, 5: 105-116.

Lee, H. L., V. Padmanabhan, and S. Whang. 1997. The bullwhip effect in supply chains. *Sloan Management Review*, 38: 93-102.

Lefebvre, L., E. Lefebvre, E. Elia, and H. Boeck. 2005. Exploring B-to-B e-commerce adoption trajectories in manufacturing SMEs. *Technovation*, 25: 1443-1456.

Léger, P.-M., L. Cassivi, P. Hadaya, and O. Caya. 2006. Safeguarding mechanisms in a supply chain network. *Industrial Management and Data Systems*, 106: 759-777.

Levenburg, N. 2005. Does size matter? Small firms' use of e-business tools in the supply chain. *Electronic Markets*, 15(2): 94-105.

Levin, A. M., I. P. Levin, and C. E. Heath. 2003. Product category dependent consumer preferences for online and offline shopping features and their influence on multi-channel retail alliances. *Journal of Electronic Commerce Research,* 4(3): 85-93.

Levy, M., P. Powell, and P. Yetton. 2001. SMEs: aligning IS and the strategic context. *Journal of Information Technology*, 16(1): 133-144.

Lewin, J. E., and W. J. Johnston. 1997. Relationship marketing theory in practice: a case study. *Journal of Business Research*, 39(1): 23-31.

Li, Y., X. W. Liao, and H. Z. Lei. 2006. A knowledge management system for ERP implementation. *Systems Research and Behavioral Science*, 23(2): 157-168.

Liang, T.P., and J.S. Huang. 1998. An empirical study on consumer acceptance of products in electronic markets: a transaction cost model. *Decision Support Systems*, 24: 29-43.

Lim, N. 2003. Consumers' perceived risk: sources versus consequences.

Electronic Commerce Research and Applications, 2: 216-228.

Liu, J. Y., J. M. Tarn, and H. J. Wen. 2004. Adopting e-commerce web site operation modes - the current stage of large US firms. *Information Management and Computer Security*, 12(1): 73-90.

Liu, X., and K. K. Wei. 2003. An empirical study of product differences in consumers' e-commerce adoption behaviour. *Electronic Commerce Research and Applications*, 2: 229-239.

Locke, S. 2004. ICT Adoption and SME Growth in New-Zealand. *Journal of American Academy of Business,* Cambridge, 4(1/2): 93-102.

Loforte Robeiro, F., and P. E. D. Love. 2003. Value creation through an e-business strategy: implication for SMEs in construction. *Construction Innovation*, 3(1): 3-14.

Loh, T. C., and S. C. L. Koh. 2004. Critical elements for a successful enterprise resource planning implementation in small and medium-sized enterprise. *International Journal of Production Research*, 42(17): 3433-3455.

Lonsdale, C. 2001. Locked-in to supplier dominance: on the danger of asset specificity for the outsourcing decision. *Journal of Supply Chain Management*, 37: 22-27.

Lowengart, O., and N. Tractinsky. 2001. Differential effects of product category on shoppers' selection of web-based stores: a probabilistic modeling approach. *Journal of Electronic Commerce Research*, 2(4): 142-156.

Macdonald, S., D. Assimakopoulos, and P. Anderson. 2007. Education and training for innovation in SMEs: a tale of exploitation. *International Small Business Journal*, 25: 77- 95.

MacKay, N., M. Parent, and A. Gemino. 2004. A model of electronic commerce adoption by small voluntary organizations. *European Journal of Information Systems,* 13(2): 147-159.

Maguire, S., and S. C. L. Koh. 2007. The adoption of e-business and knowledge management in SMEs. *Benchmarking: An International Journal*, 14(1): 37-58

Malone, T. W., and K. Crowston. 1994. The interdisciplinary study of coordination. *ACM Computing Surveys*, 26: 87-119.

Malone, T. W., J. Yates, and R. I. Benjamin. 1987. Electronic markets and electronic hierarchies. *Communications of the ACM,* 30(6): 484-497.

Mann, C., F. Stewart. 2000. *Internet communication and qualitative research: a handbook for researching online*. London : Sage Publications.

Marchesnay, M. 2003. La petite entreprise : sortir de l'ignorance. *Revue Française de Gestion*, 29(144) : 107-118.

Markus, M. L., S. Axline, D. Petrie, and C. Tanis. 2000. Learning from adopters' experiences with ERP–successes and problems. *Journal of Information Technology*, 15(4): 245-265.

Marquez, A. C., C. Bianchi, and J. N. D. Gupta. 2004. Operational and financial effectiveness of e-collaboration tools in supply chain integration. *European Journal of Operational Research,* 159: 348-363.

Martin, R., and J. Milway. 2007. Accroître la productivité des petites et moyennes entreprises par une plus grande utilisation des technologies de l'information et des communications. *Conseil des technologies de l'information et des communications*, Canada.

Martin, L. M., and H. Matlay. 2003. Innovative use of the Internet in established small firms: The impact of knowledge management and organisational learning in accessing new opportunities. *Qualitative Market Research*, 6(1): 18-27.

McCarthy, T. M., and S. L. Golicic. 2002. Implementing collaborative forecasting to improve supply chain performance. *International Journal of Physical Distribution & Logistics Management*, 32: 431-54.

McDonald, J. F., and R. A. Moffitt. 1980. The uses of Tobit analysis. *The Review of Economics and Statistics,* 62*:* 318-321.

McGinnis, T. C., and Z. Huang. 2007. Rethinking ERP success: a new perspective from knowledge management and continuous improvement. *Information & Management*, 44(7): 626-634.

Mehrtens, J., P. B. Cragg, and A. M. Mills. 2001. A model of internet adoption by SMEs. *Information and Management,* 39:165–176.

Mentzer, J. T., W. DeWitt, J. S. Keebler, S. Min, N. W., Nix, C. D., Smith, and Z. G. Zacharia. 2001. What Is Supply Chain Management? in Mentzer, J.T. (Eds.). *Supply Chain Management.* Thousand Oaks, California: Sage Publications, 5-24.

Min, S., A. Roath, P. J. Daugherty, S. E. Genchev, H. Chen, and A. D. Arndt. 2005. Supply chain collaboration: what's happening? *The International Journal of Logistic Management*, 16: 237-256.

Moen, O., M. Gavlen, and I. Endersen. 2004. Internationalization of small, computer software firms: entry forms and market selection. *European Journal of Marketing.* 38(9/10): 1236-1252.

Montazemi, A. 2006. How they manage IT: SMEs in Canada and the U.S. *Communication of the ACM*, 49(12): 109-112.

Moore, G. C., and I. Benbasat. 1991. Development of an instrument to measure the perceptions of adopting an information technology innovation. *Information Systems Research*, 2(3): 192-222.

Mudambi, S. 2002. Branding importance in business-to-business market – three buyer clusters. *Industrial Marketing Management*, 31: 525-533.

Munkvold, B. E., I. Zigurs. 2005. Integration of e-collaboration technologies: research opportunities and challenges. *International Journal of e-Collaboration,* 1: 1-24.

Muscatello, J. R., and D. H. Parente. 2006. Enterprise resource planning (ERP): a post-implementation cross-case analysis. *Information Resources Management Journal*, 19(3): 61-80.

Muscatello, J. R., and I. J. Small Chen. 2003. Implementing enterprise resource planning (ERP) systems in small and midsize manufacturing firms. *International Journal of Operations & Production Management*, 23(8): 850-871.

Musaji, Y. 2005. ERP Postimplementation problems. *Information Systems Audit and Control Associations.* Journal Online, Vol. 4: 1-9. http://www.itgi.org/Template.cfm?Section=Home&Template=/ContentManagement/ContentDisplay.cfm&ContentID=26149

Newkirk, H. E., A. L. Lederer, and A. M. Johnson. 2008. Rapid business and IT change: drivers for strategic information systems planning? *European Journal of Information Systems*, 17(3): 198-218.

Nicolaou, A. I., and S. Bhattacharya. 2006. Organizational performance effects of ERP systems usage: the impact of post-implementation changes. *International Journal of Accounting Information Systems*, 7(1): 18-35.

Nunnally, J.C. 1978. *Psychometric theory*. New-York: McGraw-Hill BookCompany.

OCDE. 2004. *ICT, E-Business and SMEs*. Paris: OECD.

OECD. 2002. *Information Technology Outlook.* Paris: OECD

Okoli, C., and S. D. Pawlowski. 2004. The Delphi method as a research tool: an example, design considerations and applications. *Information & Management*, 42: 15-29.

Olsen, K., and P. Saetre. 2007. IT for niche companies: is an ERP system the solution? *Info Systems Journal*, 17(1): 37-58.

Osterwalder, A., Y. Pigneur, and C. L. Tucci. 2005. *Clarifying Business Models: Origins, Present and Future of the Concept*. Communications of the Association for Information Systems, May, Vol.16: 1-25.

Palanisamy, R. 2007. Organizational culture and knowledge management in ERP implementation: an empirical study. *Journal of Computer Information Systems*, 48(2): 100-120.

Palmer, J. W., and M. L. Markus. 2000. The performance impacts of quick response and strategic alignment in specialty retailing. *Information Systems Research*, 11(3): 241-260.

Pan, S. L., S. Newell, J. Huang, and R. D. Galliers. 2006. Overcoming knowledge management challenges during ERP implementation: the need to integrate and share different types of knowledge. *Journal of American Society for Information Science and Technology*, 58(3): 404-419.

Pavic, S., S. C. L. Koh, M. Simpson, and J. Padmore. 2007. Could e-business create a competitive advantage in UK SMEs? *Benchmarking*, 14(3): 320-351.

Peppard, J., and K. Breu. 2003. Beyond alignment: a coevolutionary view of the information systems strategy process. Paper presented at the Twenty-Fourth International Conference on Information Systems, Date, in Seattle, USA. *Proceedings of the Twenty-Fourth International Conference on Information Systems*, 742-750.

Peterson, R. A., S. Balasubramanian, and B. J. Bronnenberg. 1997. Exploring the implications of the internet for consumer marketing. *Journal of the Academy of Marketing Science*, 25(4): 329-346.

Phau, I., and S. M. Poon. 2000. Factors influencing the types of products and services purchased over the internet. *Internet Research: Electronic Networking Applications and Policy*, 10(2): 102-113.

Pittaway, L., M. Robertson, K. Munir, D. A. Denyer and A. Neely. 2004. Networking and innovation: a systematic review of the evidence. *International Journal of Management Reviews*, 5/6(3/4): 137-168.

Poon, S. 2000. Business environment and internet commerce benefit – a small business perspective. *European Journal of Information Systems*, 9(2): 72-81.

Porter, M. 2001. Strategy and the internet. *Harvard Business Review*, 79(3): 63-78.

Powell, W. W., K. Koput, and L. Smith-Doerr. 1996. Interorganizational collaboration and the locus of innovation: networks of learning in biotechnology. *Administrative Science Quarterly*, 41:116-145.

Premkumar, G., and M. Roberts. 1999. Adoption of new information technologies in rural small businesses. *Omega: The International Journal of Management Science*, 27: 467-484.

Premkumar, G., and K. Ramamurthy. 1995. The Role of interorganizational and organizational factors on the decision mode for adoption of interorganizational Systems. *Decision Sciences*, 26, 303-336.

Prescott, M. B., and S. A. Conger. 1995. Information technology innovations: A Classification by IT Focus of Impact and Research Approach. *Data Base Advanced*, 36: 20-41.

Purvis, R. L., V. Sambamurthy, and R. W. Zmud, 2001. The assimilation of knowledge platforms in organizations: an empirical investigation. *Organization Science*, 12(2): 117-135.

Quelch, J. A., and L. R. Klein. 1996. The internet and international marketing. *Sloan Management Review*, 37(3): 60-76.

Rai, A., T. Ravichadran, and S. Samaddar. 1998. How to anticipate the internet's global diffusion. *Communication or the ACM*, 41(10): 97-106.

Ravichandran, T. 2005. Organizational assimilation of complex technologies: an empirical study of component based software development. *IEEE Transactions on Engineering Management*, 52(2): 249-268.

Raymond, L., and F. Bergeron. 2008. Enabling the business strategy of SMEs through e-business capabilities: a strategic alignment perspective. *Industrial Management & Data Systems*, 108(5): 577-595.

Raymond, L., and A.M. Croteau. 2006. Enabling the strategic development of SMEs through advanced manufacturing systems – a configurational perspective. *Industrial Management & Data Systems*, 106(7): 1012-1032.

Raymond, L., F. Bergeron, and S. Blili. 2005. The assimilation of e-business in manufacturing SMEs: determinants and effects on growth and internationalization. *Electronic Markets*, 15(2): 106-118.

Raymond, L., F. Bergeron, C. Leclerc, and M. Gladu. 1998. Impact de la congruence des TI sur la performance des PME : une étude empirique. Paper presented at the 6ème Conférence Européenne sur les SI, in Aix-en-Provence, France. *Actes du 6eme Congrès Européen sur les Systèmes d'Information,* 173-187.

Raymond, L., G. Paré, and F. Bergeron. 1995. Matching information technology and organization structure: an empirical study with implications for performance. *European Journal of Information Systems*, 10(4): 3-16.

Raz, O., and A. Goldberg. 2006. How to make IT work: cognitive perspectives for better information technology performance. *European Management Journal*, 24(2/3): 199-205.

Reekers, N., and S. Smithson. 1994. EDI in Germany and UK. *European Journal of Information Systems*, 3: 169-178.

Reich, B. H., and I. Benbasat. 2000. Factors that influence the social dimension of alignment between business and information. Technology Objectives, *MIS Quarterly*, 24(1): 81-113.

Ritchie, B., and C. Brindley. 2005. ICT adoption by SMEs: implications for relationships and management. *New Technology, Work & Employment*, 20(3): 205-217.

Riggins, F. J., and T. Mukhopadyay. 1994. Interdependent benefits from interorganizational systems: opportunities for business partner reengineering.*Journal of Management Information Systems*, 11: 37-57.

Rivard, S., L. Raymond, and D. Verreault. 2006. Resource-based view and competitive strategy: An integrated model of the contribution of information technology to firm performance. *Journal of Strategic Information Systems*, 15(1): 29-50.

Rogers, E.M. 1995. *Diffusion of innovation.* 4th edition, New York: The Free Press.

Roland, J., T. Lawver, and T. Randery. 2000. *E-sales: the web is not enough – how to realize profitable growth from your multi-channel go-to-market approach*. McKinsey Marketing Practice.

Rougès, J-F., D. Poulin, S. D'Amours, and B. Montreuil. 2007. Les technologies de l'information et de la communication, levier de performance pour les PME, revue d'une littérature ambiguë. Paper presented at the *eCommerce & Gouvernance de l'Internet (ECIG 2007)*, October 19-20, in Sousse, Tunisia.

Sabath, R. E., and J. Fontanella. 2002. The unfulfilled promise of supply chain collaboration. *Supply Chain Management Review*, 6: 24-29.

Sabherwal, R., R. Hirschheim, and T. Goles. 2001. The dynamics of alignment: insights from a punctuated equilibrium model. *Organization Science*, 12(2): 179-197.

Sabherwal, R., and Y. E. Chan. 2001. Alignment between business and IS strategies: a study of prospectors, analysers and defenders. *Information Systems Research*, 12(1): 11-43.

Sabherwal, S. 2000. Price Discovery for Dually Traded Securities: Evidence from The United States –listed Canadian Stocks. Ph.D. Diss., Georgia Institute of Technology, USA.

Saeed, K., M. K. Malhotra, and V. Grover. 2005. Examining the impact of inter-Organizational systems on process efficiency and sourcing leverage in buyer-supplier dyads. *Decision Sciences*, 36: 365-396.

Salmeron, J., and S. Bueno. 2006. An information technologies and information systems industry-based classification in small and medium-sized enterprises: An institutional view. *European Journal of Operational Research*, 173(3): 1012-1025.

Samaddar, S., S. Nargundkar, and M. Daley. 2006. Inter-organizational information sharing: the role of supply network configuration and partner characteristics. *European Journal of Operational Research*, 174(2): 744-765.

Samaddar, S., S. Nargundkar, and S. Chatterjee. 2002. E-market infrastructure planning and internet growth. Paper presented at the 8th Americas Conference on Information systems, in Dallas, Texas. *Proceedings of the Eighth American Conference on Information*

System, 721-729.

Santarelli, E., and S. D'Altri. 2001. The Diffusion of e-Commerce at the Firm Level: Theoretical Implications and Empirical Evidence. Working paper, AMS Acta University of Bologna.

Santhanam, R., E. Hartono. 2003. Issues in linking information technology capability to firm performance. *MIS Quaterly*, 27(1): 125-153.

Saunders, C. S., and S. Clark. 1992. EDI adoption and implementation: a focus on interorganizational linkages. *Information Resources Management Journal,* 5: 9-19.

Schaupp, L. C., and F. Bélanger. 2005. A conjoint analysis of online consumer satisfaction. *Journal of Electronic Commerce Research*, 6(2): 95-111.

Schlemmer, F., and B. Webb. 2006. The Impact of Strategic Assets on Financial Performance and on Internet Performance. *Electronics Markets*, 16(4): 371-385.

Schubert, P., U. Leimstoll. 2007. Importance and use of information technology in small and medium-sized companies. *Electronic Markets*, 17(1): 38-55.

Scott, W.R. 1995. *Institutions and organizations*. California: Sage Publications.

Scupola, A. 2002. Adoption Issues of Business-to-Business Internet Commerce in European SMEs. Paper presented at the 35th Annual Hawaii International Conference on System Science (HICSS), January 7-10, Hawaii. *Proceedings of the 35th Annual Hawaii International Conference on System Science,* Volume 7: 165.

Selhofer, H. 2004. *The european e business report 2004 edition. A portrait of e-business in 10 sectors of the EU economy.* 3rd Synthesis Report of the e-Business W@tch. European Commission. Enterprise Directorate General, Bonn.

Seng, C., E. Zannes, and W. Pace. 2002. The contributions of knowledge management to workplace learning. *Journal of Workplace Learning,* 14(4): 138-147.

Shehab, E. M., M. W. Sharp, L. Supramanian, and T. A. Spedding. 2004. Enterprise resource planning: an integrative review. *Business Process Management Journal*, 10(4): 359-386.

Sheppard, B. H., and D. M. Sherman. 1998. The grammars of trust: a model and general implications. *Academy of Management Review*, 23: 422-437.

Sherif, K., and H. Maha. 2004. King Hotel Goes Online: The case of a *medium enterprise* in using eCommerce. *Journal of Electronic Commerce in Organizations*, 2(4): 101-115.

Simatupang, T. M., and R. Sridharan. 2005. The collaboration index: a measure for supply chain collaboration. *International Journal of Physical Distribution and Logistics Management*, 35: 44-62.

Simpson, M., and A. J. Docherty. 2004. E-commerce adoption support and advice for UK SMEs. *Journal of Small Business and Enterprise Development*, 11(3): 315-328.

Skjevdal, R., and L. H. VIK. 2004. SEAMATE: deliverable 4.1, SINTEF Industrial Management, Economics and logistics, Trondheim, Norway.

Somers, T. M., and K. G. Nelson. 2004. A taxonomy of players and activities across the ERP project life cycle. *Information and Management*, 41(3): 257-278.

Somers, T. M., and K. G. Nelson. 2003. The impact of strategy and integration mechanisms on enterprise resource planning system value: empirical evidence from manufacturing firms. *European Journal of Operational Research*, 146(2): 315-338.

Srinivasan, S. 2004. Role of trust in e-business success. *Information Management and Computer Security*, 12(1): 66-72.

Stank, T. P., P. J. Daugherty, and C. W. Autry. 1999. Collaborative planning: supporting automatic replenishment programs. *Supply Chain Management: An International Journal*, 4: 75-85.

Stansfield, M., and K. Grant. 2003. An investigation into issues influencing the use of the internet and electronic commerce among small-medium size enterprises. *Journal of Electronic Commerce Research*, 4(1): 15-26.

St-Pierre, J., C. Schmitt, and L. Raymond. 2007. Collaboration entre chercheurs et praticiens pour la production de connaissances scientifiques et opérationnelles: réflexions autour d'une expérience canadienne. Paper presented at the *Second International Conference of the Research Methods Division of the Academy of Management and the ISEOR,* 1-14 (Cederom).

Stuart, I., D. McCutcheon, R. Handfiled, R. McLachlin, and D. Samson. 2002. Effective case research in operations management: a process perspective. *Journal of Operations Management*, 20(5): 419-433.

Subramaniam, C., and M. J. Shaw. 2002. A study on the value and impact of B2B e-commerce: the case of web-based procurement. *International Journal of Electronic Commerce*, 6(4): 41-72.

Sveiby, K-E. 2001. A knowledge-based theory of the firm to guide strategy formulation. *Journal of Intellectual Capital*, 2(4): 344-358.

Swatman, P. M. C., and P. A. Swatman. 1991. Electronic Data Interchange: Organizational Opportunity, Not Technical Problem, in B. Srinivasan and J. Zeleznikow (Eds.), *Databases in the 1990's: 2,*

Singapore: World Scientific Press, 354-374.

Szulanski, G. 2000. The process of knowledge transfer: a diachronic analysis of stickiness. *Organizational Behavior and Human Decision Processes*, 82(1): 9-27.

Tallon, P. P 2008. A process-oriented perspective on the alignment of information technology and business strategy. *Journal of Management Information Systems,* 24(3): 227-268.

Tan, B. L., N. K. H. Tang, and P. L. Forrester. 2004. Application of QFD for e-Business planning. *Production Planning & Control,* 15(8): 802-818.

Tavakolian, H. 1989. Linking the information technology structure with organizational competitive strategy: a survey. *MIS Quarterly*, 13(3): 309-315.

Teng, J. T. C., V. Grover, and W. Güttler. 2002. Information technology innovations: general diffusion patterns and its relationships to innovation characteristics. *IEEE Transactions on Engineering Management*, 49(1): 13-27.

Teo, H. H., K. K. Wei, and I. Benbasat. 2003. Predicting intention to adopt interorganizational linkages: an institutional perspective. *MIS Quarterly*, 27(1): 19-49.

Teo, T. S. H., and W. R. King. 1996. Assessing the impact of integrating business planning and IS planning. *Information and Management*, 30(6): 309-322.

Tessier, S., D. Lagace. 2003. Productivité et activité en R&D des entreprises manufacturières québécoises. *Gestion*, 28(2): 92-103.

Tetteh, E., and J. Burn. 2001. Global strategies for SMe-business: applying the SMALL framework. *Logistics Information Management*, 14(1/2): 171-181.

Thomas, B., G. Packham, C. Miller, and D. Brooksbank. 2004. The use of web sites for SME innovation and technology support services in wales. *Journal of Small Business and Enterprise Development*, 11(3): 400-407.

Tobin, J. 1958. Estimation of relationships for limited dependent variables. *Econometrica*, 26: 26-36.

Tornatzky, L. G., and R. J. Klein. 1982. Innovation characteristics and innovation adoption implementation: a meta-analysis of findings. *IEEE Transactions on Engineering Management*, 29: 28045.

Tornatzky, L. G., and M. Fleischer. 1990. *The processes of technological innovation*. Massachusetts:Lexington Books.

Towill, D. R., N. M. Naim, and J. Wikner. 1992. Industrial dynamics simulation models in the design of supply chains. *International*

Journal of Physical Distribution and Logistics Management, 22: 3-13.

Treacy, M., and F. Wiersema. 1997. *The Discipline of Market Leaders: Choose your Customers, Narrow your Focus, Dominate your Market.* New York: Perseus books.

Tsao, H-Y., and K. H-C. Lin. 2004. An investigation of critical success factors in the adoption of B2BEC by Taiwanese companies. *Journal of American Academy of Business,* Cambridge, 5(1/2): 198-202.

Tsao, H-Y., and K. H-C. Lin. 2001. A two-level approach to establishing a marketing strategy in the electronic marketplace. Paper presented at the 34th Annual Hawaii International Conference on System Science, in Hawaii. *Proceedings of the 34th Annual Hawaii International Conference on System Science.*

Umble, E. J., R. R. Haft, and M. M. Umble. 2003. Enterprise resource planning: implementation procedures and critical success factors. *European Journal of Operations Research*, 146(2): 241-257.

Ure, J. 2002. Modelling critical mass for e-commerce: the case of Hong Kong. *Electronic Commerce Research*, 2: 87-111.

U.S. Commercial Service And U.S. Department Of State 2006. Profile of Quebec's Furniture Manufacturing Industry, http://commercecan.ic.gc.ca/scdt/bizmap/interface2.nsf/vDownload/IMI_6919/$file/X_7077465.PDF last accessed August 21, 2007.

Van den Poel, D., and J. Leunis. 1999. Consumer acceptance of the internet as a channel of distribution. *Journal of Business Research*, 45: 249-256.

Van de Ven, A. H., R. Drazin. 1985. The concept of fit in contingency theory. *Research in Organizational Behavior*, 7: 333-365

Van Horne, C., J-M. Frayret, and D. Poulin. 2005. Knowledge management in the forest products industry: the role of centers of expertise. *Computers and Electronics in Agriculture*, 47 (3): 167-184.

Van Horne, C., D. Poulin, R. Landry, and J-M. Frayret. 2007. Academic research centres as sources of services and technologies: towards taxonomy. Paper presented at the XVII International RESER Conference, September 13-15, in Tampere, Finland.

Vemuri, V. K., and S. C. Palvia. 2006. Improvement in operational efficiency due to ERP systems implementation: truth or myth. *Information Resources Management Journal,* 19(2): 18-37.

Venkatraman, N. 1989. The concept of fit in strategy research: toward verbal and statistical correspondence. *Academy of Management Review*, 14(3): 423-444.

—. 1989. Strategic orientation of business enterprises: the construct, dimensionality, and measurement. *Management Science,* 35(8): 942-

963.

Ventatesh, V., M. G. Morris, G. B. Davis, and F. D. Davis. 2003. User acceptance of information technology: toward unified view. *MIS Quarterly*, 27(3): 76-80.

Vijayasarathy, L. R. 2002. Product characteristics and internet shopping intention. *Internet Research: Electronic Networking Applications and Policy*, 12(5): 411-426.

Wade, M., D. Johnston, and R. Mclean. 2004. Exploring the net impact of internet business solution adoption on SME performance. *International Journal of Electronic Business*, 2(4): 336-351.

Watson, B. P. 2007. Is strategic alignment still a priority? *CIO Insight*, (10): 37-39.

Weible, R., and J. Wallace. 1998. Cyber research: the impact of the internet on data collection. *Marketing Research*, 10: 19-31.

Wetzels, M. G. M. 2003. To accept or not to accept - is that the question? Inaugural lecture Technische Universiteit Eindhoven, June 6.

Wikner, J., D. R. Towill, and M. Naim. 1991. Smoothing supply chain dynamics. *International Journal of Production Economics*, 22: 231-248.

Williamson, O. E. 1975. *Markets and hierarchies: analysis and antitrust implication.* New York: The Free Press.

Winklhofer, H., K. Houghton, and T. Chesney. 2007. How advanced are websites of SME exporters? An investigation into drivers and inhibitors. *Advances in International Marketing*, 17: 395-426.

Wright, M., C. Upritchard, and A. Lewis. 1997. A validation of the bass model of new product diffusion in New Zealand. *Marketing Bulletin*, (8): 15-29.

Wu, J., and Y. Wang. 2006. Measuring ERP success: the ultimate users' view. *International Journal of Operations & Production Management*, 26(8): 882-903.

Wu, W-Y., C-Y. Chiang, Y-J. Wu, and H-J. Tu. 2004. The Influencing factors of commitment and business integration on supply chain management. *Industrial Management + Data Systems*, 104(3/4): 322.

Yang, C., P. Ting, and C. Wei. 2006. A Study of the Factors Impacting ERP System Performance – from the User's Perspectives. *Journal of American Academy of Business*, 8(2): 161-166.

Yin, R. K. 2003. *Case Study Research: Design and Methods*. 3rd edition, London: Sage Publications.

—. 1994. *Case study research: Design and Methods*.2nd edition, Thousand Oaks, CA.: Sage Publications.

Zheng, J., N. Caldwell, C. Harland, P. Powell, and M. Woerndl. 2004.

Small firms and e-business: cautiousness, contingency and cost-benefit. *Journal of Purchasing and Supply Management*, 10(1): 27-39.

Zhou, L., W. K. Chiang, and D. Zhang. 2004. Discovering rules for predicting customers' attitude toward internet retailers. *Journal of Electronic Commerce Research*, 5(4): 228-238.

Zmud, R. W. 1982. Diffusion of modern software practices: influence of centralization and formalization. *Management Science*, 28: 1421-1431.

Websites

Global 100. 2007. Manufacturing business technology. *Reed Business Information.* http://www.mbtmag.com/info/CA6433117.html. Last visited August 29th, 2007.

Industry Canada Website. 2002. The Canadian furniture Industry: An Overview. CSIL Publication "World Furniture – International Markets Review. September. http://strategis.ic.gc.ca/eic/site/furniture-meuble.nsf/en/rf03598e.html. Last accessed August 21, 2007.

Information Economy -- Sector Definitions Based on the International Standard Industry Classification (ISIC 4), DSTI/ICCP/IIS (2006) 2/FINAL, Organisation for Economic Co-operation and Development. http://www.oecd.org/dataoecd/49/17/38217340.pdf. Last visited March 9th, 2009.

Information Technology Outlook, 2008, Organisation for Economic Co-operation and Development. http://www.oecd.org/document/20/0,3343,en_2649_33757_41892820_1_1_1_1,00.html. Last visited March 9th, 2009.

Verespej, M. 2005. Supply chain collaboration. *Frontline Solutions,* available at www. frontlinetoday.com (accessed August 2005).

CONTRIBUTORS

François Bergeron is a full professor of IT Governance at Télé-université, UQAM (Canada). His areas of research and consulting are in IT governance, strategic alignment, strategic planning of IT personnel and the contribution of IT to business performance. Prior to UQAM, he was a professor of IT at Université Laval (Canada), and founding director of RGTI, a multi-university research group studying IT management. He has published extensively in journals such as *MIS Quarterly, European Journal of Information Systems, Journal of Strategic Information Systems,* and *Information & Management*. He holds an MBA and a M.Sc. in Economics from Université Laval and a PhD from the Anderson School of Management at UCLA (USA).

Sébastien Caisse is a business executive with over sixteen years of experience in strategic management, entrepreneurship, talent networking and academia. He holds a PhD in business design from Université Laval (Canada) and works in the video games industry. He is passionate about all things related to storytelling, most notably sharing insights and learning from his audience.

Luca Canetta is a senior researcher and lecturer at the Institute CIM for Sustainable Innovation of the University of Applied Sciences of Southern Switzerland. He received his PhD in Demand Modeling and Operations Management from EPFL (Ecole Polytechnique Fédérale de Lausanne – Switzerland) His main research interests are production system robustness, customer behavior analysis, and demand modeling. He has published several papers in various journals and international conferences.

Naoufel Cheikhrouhou is the head of the Operations Management group at EPFL (Ecole Polytechnique Fédérale de Lausanne – Switzerland). His main research interests are in the areas of modeling, simulation and optimization of supply networks, the identification and integration of human factors in production management and the reduction of management complexity in logistics and services, for which Dr. Cheikhrouhou received the Burbidge Award in 2003.

Yan Cimon is an assistant professor of strategy at the Faculty of Business Administration at Université Laval (Canada). He holds a PhD from HEC Montréal (Canada). He is a member of the Interuniversity Research Center on Enterprise Networks, Logistics and Transportation (CIRRELT). His research focuses on strategic management, networks and the management of technology. Among other outlets, his research has been published in *Decision Support Systems* and the *Journal of Knowledge Management*.

Sophie D'Amours is a full professor in Industrial engineering at the Faculty of Science and Engineering at Université Laval (Canada). She holds a PhD in Engineering Mathematics from the École Polytechnique de Montréal (Canada), as well as an M.B.A. and a B.Sc. in Mechanical Engineering from Université Laval. She is currently General Director of FOR@C Research Consortium and full time researcher. She holds a Canada Research Chair in planning sustainable forest networks. She is also codirector of the CIRRELT Research Center. Her research interests are in collaborative planning, agent-based decisions support systems, supply chain management and e-business. She applies most of her work to the forest products industry.

Jean-Marc Frayret is an assistant professor of industrial engineering at École Polytechnique de Montréal (Canada). Over the past eight years, Dr. Frayret worked in the field of logistics in the forest products sector. His research interests focus on designing systems to support decision making in the domain of manufacturing and logistics operations planning. For over 10 years he has studied the complex problems of coordination and cooperation in supply chain management, to which he applied the tools of operations research and multi-agent systems for the design of advanced collaborative planning and scheduling systems.

Rémy Glardon is a professor at EPFL (École Polytechnique Fédérale de Lausanne – Switzerland). He is the founder and director of the Laboratory for Production Management and Processes. He has a MS in Mechanical Engineering and a PhD in Materials Science from EPFL. After his graduate study at EPFL, he spent several years as a postdoc at UC-Berkeley (USA). He then joined industry and occupied several management positions in production, logistics and operations management. His main research interests are in the design and operation of value adding networks, to skills management and to the integration of human aspects in these complex systems. Professor Glardon has initiated and completed several research and consulting projects with private companies in these areas.

Pierre Hadaya is a professor in the Department of Management and Technology at École des Sciences de la Gestion de l'Université du Québec à Montréal (UQAM) (Canada). He holds a bachelor in electronical enginnering and a PhD in Management of Technology from École Polytechnique de Montréal (Canada). His main research interests lie at the intersection of information technology management, business strategy, and interorganizational design.

Hedi Kaffel obtained a PhD in 2001 at Université Laval (Canada) and a Master's degree in 1996 at Université de Sherbrooke (Canada). He received more than 6 scholarships and recognitions of excellence. He was an assistant professor at the Engineering faculty of Moncton University (Canada) between July 2001 and August 2002. He is currently working at the CRIQ (Quebec Industrial Research Center). He is leading a project concerning network implementation of knowledge management in either corporate or industrial networking.

Rafa Kouki holds a PhD in Administration Sciences from Université Laval (Canada), an MBA and a B.Com. in management information systems and operations management from the University of Ottawa (Canada). She is a member of the Interuniversity Research Centre on Enterprise Networks, Logistics and Transportation (CIRRELT). Her current research interests include ERP systems assimilation and success assessment, global IT management and strategies for integration and coordination of business processes.

Benoit Montreuil is a full professor of operations and decisions systems at Université Laval (Canada). He is a professional industrial engineer with a PhD (1982) from the Georgia Institute of Technology (USA). He holds the Canada Research Chair in Enterprise Engineering. His main research interests lie in developing concepts, methodologies and technologies for creating, transforming and enabling businesses and value creation networks to sustainably thrive in a fast evolving world. He has extensive advisory, entrepreneurial and collaborative research experience with industry.

Robert Pellerin is associate professor in the Department of Mathematics and Industrial Engineering at École Polytechnique de Montréal. He holds degrees in engineering management (B.Eng.) and industrial engineering (PhD). He is a member of the Interuniversity Research Center on Enterprise Networks, Logistics and Transportation (CIRRELT). His research interests include enterprise system adoption, implementation, and integration. He has published several papers in various journals and international conferences.

Diane Poulin is a full professor of management at Université Laval (Canada). She holds a PhD in management from the École Polytechnique de Paris (France), a Master's degree in public administration from the École d'administration publique du Québec and a Master's degree in sociology from the Université de Montréal (Canada). She has taught in American and European universities as a visiting professor. She is a member of the Interuniversity Research Center on Enterprise Networks, Logistics and Transportation (CIRRELT), and of the FOR@C Research Consortium. Her areas of research and consulting are mainly in strategy and networking.

Jean Francois Rougès is a senior consultant in change management. In juxtaposition, he is currently completing his PhD at Université Laval (Canada). He is a member of the CIRRELT (Interuniversity Research Centre on Enterprise Networks, Logistics and Transportation). His thesis is under the direction of Professors Diane Poulin and Benoit Montreuil. His research focuses on the strategic opportunity of ICT for SMEs and is funded by CED (Canada Economic Development) and *Emploi Québec* with the ambition to foster the strategic use of ICT within SMEs throughout the Province of Quebec.

Constance Van Horne is an assistant Professor in the College of Business Sciences at Zayed University, Abu Dhabi (UAE). She received her PhD and MBA from Université Laval (Canada), and holds a Bachelor's degree in History from the University of Victoria (Canada). Her research interests include innovation process management, the transfer of knowledge and technology developed in centres of expertise to industry and the forest products industry. Her work has been published in *Forest Policy and Economics* and *Computers and Electronics in Agriculture.*

INDEX